RADIO DAZE

Book, Music & Lyrics by

Amy Shojai & Frank Steele

Performance rights for all materials contained herein
must be obtained from Shojai & Steele Plays
http://amyshojai.com/plays
Copyright © 2018-2019 by Amy Shojai, Frank Steele
ALL RIGHTS RESERVED/Music ASCAP Registered

RADIO DAZE

A 1940s Musical
In Two Acts

903-868-1022 or 903-893-2039
ALL MUSIC REGISTERED VIA ASCAP

FURRY MUSE
PUBLISHING
PO BOX 1904, SHERMAN TX 75090

DIRECTOR'S NOTES

RADIO DAZE is a funny and often touching homage to the late 1940s. The story unfolds in the failing WPDQ radio station. The owner, Bob Hope (the one from Schenectady) is ready to cut his losses and sell out to the latest fad—television. A motley crew of staff, has-been movie stars, and strangers off the street come together to try and save the station--and fail miserably to hilarious effect.

RADIO DAZE is the perfect early Valentine's "date night" or family-friendly-evening-out event. The two-hour show will leave you laughing, humming catchy tunes, and hugging your loved ones close.

PRODUCTION HISTORY

A table reading of the completed **RADIO DAZE** was first performed January 3, 2019 at HOPE ON HOUSTON, 901 E. Houston St., Sherman, Texas. The show was cast by invitation, and the book and songs written specifically for the originating talents.

RADIO DAZE full production was first staged and performed February February 7, 8, 9, 2019 at The Rialto Theater, 426 West Main Street, Denison, TX (www.TheRialtoTheater.net). Special thanks to Sherman Community players, Mike Marlow, and Denison Calvary Baptist Church.

PRODUCTION & CASTING NOTES

RADIO DAZE features a cast of 6 men and 6 women. This is an ensemble show, with no specific stars. The family-friendly script is appropriate for any age performer, from high school to professional venues.

There are no specific age-casting requirements. SNAZZY, ROB, WILADINE and POLLY may be any age. However, DOTTIE should be the youngest, and PEARL should seem younger than her uncle BOB. The remaining cast of IRVING, BENNY, BOB, DIZZY and BARRY should be played by more mature actors.

VOCAL AND MOVEMENT REQUIREMENTS

The character playing IRVING has two short solo lines in the opening song and sings in chorus numbers. All other characters sing featured solos and/or ensemble numbers.

There are opportunities for choreographed movement or 1940s-style dance breaks within some songs. This is not required and the show can be performed without.

Music is predominantly big band styles of the 1940s. Multiple verses offer feature solo line opportunities. Most songs are easy mid-range tenor and alto lines. The exceptions (SNAZZY and SPONSORS songs) may be sung up or down in the octave most comfortable for the actor.

Company numbers require two- to four-part harmonies, often written as "rounds" or combinations of melody lines. This keeps learning music simple for non-music-readers. A piano score for rehearsal is available, with show performance using a CD with full orchestration; a rehearsal piano/vocal CD can be provided. Vocal ranges from baritone (from low B) to soprano (to high F).

VIDEO PROJECTIONS & AUDIO CUES

Video projections partnered with audio orchestrations enhance several of the songs or set the scene. These are available in the licensing package but are optional.

OPENING VIDEO: Static picture of radio station building, cross-fades into hand opening door, with orchestration accompaniment for RADIO DAZE song.

OUTSIDE: Static picture of station building projected during Act 1 Scene 6, in lieu of a set change.

SPONSORS: Orchestration partnered with video, a series of 1940 products mentioned in lyrics.

FAMOUS: Orchestration partnered with video, pictures of well-known actors mentioned in lyrics.

JINGLE: A xylophone plays the station chimes, followed by each call-letter "flying" in to spell WPDQ-RADIO DAZE as 4-part voices sing the jingle. This is projected/played many times during show and characters sing along.

SOUND EFFECTS: Like radio shows of the past, sound effects are part of the two script samples presented within the RADIO DAZE show. These may be produced live by ROB, or the actor can mime producing pre-recorded cues run from the sound board. For instance, if the JINGE projection isn't used, chimes may be played "live" from ROB's sound effects and actors sing a capella.

SET, COSTUMES & PROPS

SET: A unit set may be built—perhaps set on wheels to rotate and transform into scene/spaces used: OUTSIDE, 3 OFFICES, GREEN ROOM, SOUND STUDIO. Or, as in the premier of RADIO DAZE, an open set staged simply with furniture and area lights may be used, moving the Standing Mics down center stage during the sound stage scenes.

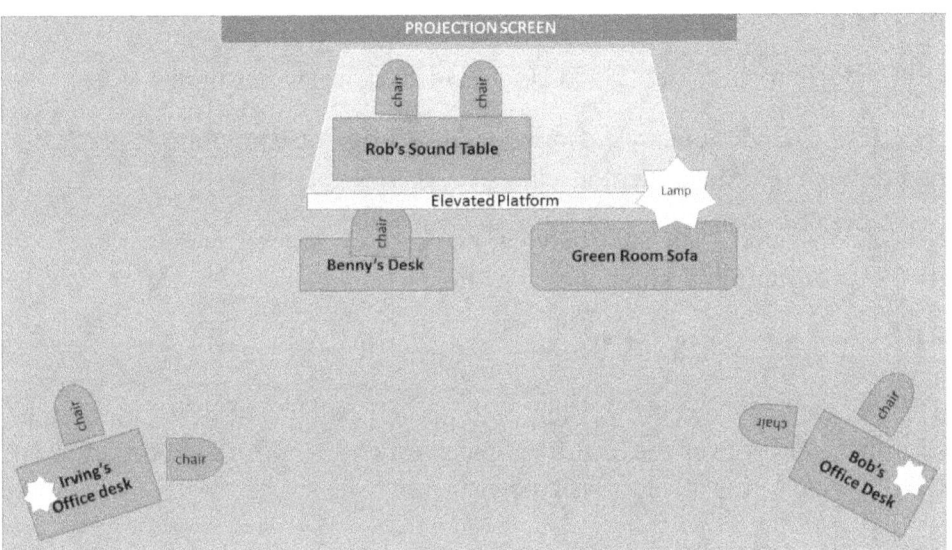

COSTUMES:

Costumes should suggest the character type, and reflect the era 1949. For instance, women should accessorize with hats, purses, and gloves, when appropriate.

MEN BASICS: Black pants, white shirts, different tie for each act, loafers or Oxfords, hats.

WOMEN BASICS: A-line dress with shoulder pads, different outfit or each act. Either 40s style wig, or hair fixed in "victory rolls" styles. Penny loafers or low-heel character shoes.

CHARACTER SPECIFICS:

DOTTIE: Dress, hat, gloves, purse Act 1: Man's black fedora with press badge, slacks and blouse for Act 2.

PEARL: High waist wide legged 40s style pants and top, different each act.

WILADINE: Overalls, 'do-rag (like Rosie-the-Riviter) for Act 1; beautiful dress for Act 2.

ROSIE: A different pencil skirt and jacket set for Act 1 and Act 2, with hat, gloves, purse. She's a business woman, very proper.

PEPPERS: Different dress, gloves, hat, purse for Act 1 and Act 2. A different color (same style) wig for PEDRO and PATTY, actress may wear own hair for POLLY.

DIZZY: 1920s-30s hair style and movie star gown (she lives on past glory) with long gloves, "fascinator" hat, boa for Act 1. 1940s dress, hat, gloves for Act 2.

BOB: Basic for Act 1 & 2, add Hawaiian shirt, straw hat final scene.

BARRY: Tuxedo (old style, from 20s-30s), bright ascot, white Panama hat, bad reddish (Cordovan) color wig

SNAZZY: Loud "salesman" outfit, such as checkered coat with lots of pockets for samples, outrageous bow tie.

PROPS & SET DRESSING

The show takes place in 1949 and the station is shabby at best. Borrowed furniture works, even makeshift set pieces such as an ironing board for ROB's sound props table. Basic needs follow:

4 Desks
2 telephones, 1 telephone hand set.
2-3 desk lamps, 1 floor lamp
5 desk chairs
Sofa
Coat/hat rack
Coffee table or side table
Old style typewriter (Underwood preferred)
Various period mics, desk top and floor stands
Percolator and coffee cups
Magazine or newspaper with ROSIE headshot
Desk stuff: Note pads, yellow legal pads, pencils, etc.
Dictionary, various books
Various radio sound effects items on ironing board or long table
Cleaning rags, feather duster, bucket, mop, broom
Salesman props
Shoe polish kit & shoe polish tins

CHARACTER BREAKDOWNS (6 M/6 W)

IRVING IRVING LIPSCHITZ (Bass): The radio station director has never had any other job. "My dad worked in same factory for 47 years, died on the job, lucky stiff, and never had to worry about changing career. Radio goes away, I got nuthin!" Sings in chorus and a solo line in opening RADIO DAZE.

BOB HOPE (from Shibogen) (Tenor): Radio station owner worries WPDQ is losing money. He's never had time for a wife, sank all his energy and dreams into the station. With that gone, he has nothing left—and it's too late to start something new. Song feature, duet WHEN I MET YOU.

WILADINE YORK (Soprano): Bob's assistant fell in love with PDQ-Radio during factory shifts but lost her job to returning serviceman. BOB hired her as first "Girl Friday" and she's eternally grateful…and smitten, but he doesn't notice her 'that way.' She knows everything that's going on, DOES everything is the behind-the-scenes glue holding everything together. Song features trio SPONSORS and duet WHEN I MET YOU.

PEARL REMINGTON (Soprano): Script writer and BOB's niece, she's writing the great American novel. An artiste and free spirit, she's in charge of her own destiny—if only she had the funds. Uncle BOB promises a year paid to a writer retreat if she produces great radio script that saves the station. Song features solo HUNTING FOR MY MUSE, duet PARTNERS.

DOTTIE SPLENDOR (Mezzo): IRVING'S "girl Friday" assistant, this is her first real job working for just the experience. She wants a career and sets her sights on being a news reporter. "If ladies can rivet airplanes, they can nail news stories, too." Song features trio SPONSORS and solo NEWS FLASH.

BENNY KORNBLAT (Tenor): Longtime news guy, he's frantic to keep job, never worked anywhere else. His writing is better than on-air delivery, and he's a curmudgeon who's always worked alone. He's offended to think a woman could do his job. Song features solo MAKE A DIFFERENCE and duet PARTNERS.

ROB BERNSTEIN (Baritone): As a professional sound effects man, he loves making weird noises. He knew it was his destiny when he won the nose whistle contest in 5th grade. "I make news stories more exciting. Sound effects are the punctuation of radio." Song feature NEWS FLASH.

SNAZZY MALONEY (Bass): He's a typical loud, an over-the-top pushy salesman competing for a job selling advertisements for WPDQ-Radio. A hyper, jokes a minute obnoxious character who gets on everyone's last nerve. Song feature duet SNAZZY MALONEY.

BARRYMORE "BARRY" JOHNATHAN SELDEN (Baritone): A washed up star from the silent film era, he's now a shoe polish salesman hired to get more advertisers for radio station. He'd rather be on-air talent. Rumors about television offers his chance for redemption. Song features include duet SNAZZY MALONEY, solo KINDA and duet KINDA FAMOUS.

DESDEMONA "DIZZY" NORMAN (Soprano): Hired as the "name" talent for last big script/show to save the station. She's blindsided by her ex-husband BARRY's presence. Her star is fading, she lives on past glory but wants a shot at TV to revitalize career. Song features include solo FAMOUS, reprise of RADIO DAZE and duet KINDA FAMOUS.

R. P. "ROSIE" WALTER (Alto/Contralto): Mistaken for receptionist applicant and hired by DOTTIE, she actually is a potential buyer for the station. She knows very little about broadcast business, and wants to learn from the misfits at KDP, where everyone fills in doing everything as needed (even singing ad jingles when singers quit). Song features include trio SPONSORS and solo line RADIO DAZE finale.

PEPPER SISTERS QUARTET (Soprano): One actress plays PEDRO, PATTY and POLLY (each wearing different color wig). They try unsuccessfully to get paid for past gigs. Ultimately POLLY becomes part of the WPDQ family. Song features solo SISTERS.

RADIO DAZE ORIGINAL CAST

IRVING	Frank Steele
BENNY	Gil Nelson
BOB	Mark Beardsley
WILADINE	Tammie Sims
PEARL	Theresa Littlefield
DOTTIE	Jenny Daniel
PEPPER SISTERS	Sally Hawthorne
ROB	Steven Mildward
BARRY	Keith Clark
SNAZZY	Ben Fuhr
DIZZY	Amy Shojai
ROSIE	M'Arty Burkart

PRODUCTION

Frank Steele	DIRECTOR
Amy Shojai	MUSIC
Kelly Rhoads & Debs Clark	ASSIST. DIRECTORS
Debs Clark	STAGE MANAGER
Kelly Rhoads	LIGHTS/SOUND/PROJECTION
Leah & Rachel Martin	SPOTLIGHTS
Cast	COSTUMES

SCENES & SONGS
ACT 1

Scene 1: Outside (Radio Daze)………Irving, Benny, Bob, Wila, Pearl, Dottie

Scene2: Irv Office………………….…..…..………….Irving, Dottie, Rob

Scene 3: Bob Office (Hunting-Muse)…..............…..…..Bob, Pedro, Pearl

Scene 4: Studio (Jingle) …………...........Benny, Rob, Wila, Dottie, Pearl

Scene 5: Irv Office (Sponsors)…………....…..Irving, Wila, Dottie, Rosie

Scene 6: Outside: …....…………………………………...….. Bob, Patty

Scene 7: Green Rm (Snazzy, Kinda)….Barry, Snazzy, Dottie, Pearl, Dizzy

Scene 8: Irv Office (Famous)…………..………Irving, Dottie, Dizzy, Pearl

Scene 9: Studio………………………….Benny, Rob, Snazzy, Pearl, Polly

Scene 10: Studio (Make A Difference, Radio Daze)…………….Company

ACT 2

Scene 1: Bob/Irv Offices: (When I Met You)……..Pearl, Wila, Bob, Rosie

Scene 2: Entire Set (News Flash)…………………....…Dottie, Company

Scene 3: Studio (Sisters)…………..…………....Polly, Rosie, Wila, Bob

Scene 4: Studio (Partners)…………….………….…Snazzy, Pearl, Benny

Scene 5: Irv Office (Kinda Famous)………….. Irving, Dizzy, Barry, Rosie

Scene 6: Studio ……………………………….. All but Rosie & Snazzy

Scene 7: Studio (Radio Daze, finale)….. ……………….………Company

ACT 1

Scene 1

> *AUDIO CUE of WPDQ Jingle*
>
> *SPOTLIGHT on IRVING and BENNY complaining outside WKDP studio. VIDEO PROJECTION of building.*

IRVING
Retire? You can't retire. Benny Kornblat has been the award-winning signature voice of WPDQ-RADIO forever. Not to mention, you got me my start in the biz.

BENNY
(horrible odd-funny voice) A lot changes over 30 years. Look at you! From an eager beaver salesman, now you're THE Irving Lipschitz, a big-shot radio director. Ah, reporting news used to be such a gas. Painting pictures with words tells the story. Irving, I've lost my muse.

IRVING
And I'm on a short fuse. Hang on just a while longer. Be a pal, Benny. Clam up, here comes the boss-man. Good morning, Mr. Hope. *(ingratiating)*

BOB
(suspicious) Mr. Hope? Okay Lipschitz, what gives? We've been on a first-name basis for . . .

                    BENNY
Thirty years, Bob, but who's counting. You were an outlaw when you started this place.

                    BOB
Yeah, everybody tells me that. *(sigh)* I know you're not happy. Neither am I but that's no reason to bust my chops. Inside. In my office. Immediately.

VIDEO of hand opening door segues to RADIO DAZE intro and ACTORS reappear entering BOB's office area.

RADIO DAZE

(BOB)
GOT MY PIECE OF PARADISE.
NOT MUCH TO BRAG ON,
BUT DANG, IT'S NICE.

(IRVING)
I GOT CREATIVE CONTROL,

(BENNY)
I WAS ON A GREAT ROLL,

(ALL THREE)
WHEN TELEVISION
CAME ALONG.

(BOB & BENNY)
NOW I'M HANGIN' ON--

(IRVING)
IT'S A TRANSIENT PHASE.

(BOB & BENNY)
JUST HANGIN' ON--

(IRVING)
DON'T GIVE IN TO THE CRAZE.

(ALL THREE)
IT'S FOR CERTAIN WE'RE DESERVIN'
AND DETERMINED, SO WE'RE YEARNIN'
TO KEEP EARNIN'
FROM RADIO DAZE.

Men freeze as music continues. WILADINE and PEARL enter, talking outside station door in SPOTLIGHT, music under dialogue.

PEARL
What's buzzin' cousin? So good to see you, Wiladine!

WILADINE
Pearl! You used to come around more often. The life of a big-time novelist must be exciting.

PEARL
You can't even imagine. I'm here to see Uncle Bob. Is he still cheesy as ever?

WILADINE
Yep, he's always been a tightwad. Several staff quit over late paychecks. I hate to gossip. You know I'd do anything for your Uncle Bob *(to herself)* even if he never notices me. Now he's lost his moxie. I'm picking up the slack where I can –

DOTTIE
(enters with energy) Isn't it a glorious morning, girls? Hiya Wiladine. *(to PEARL).* Are you interviewing for the new weekend receptionist position? I'm Dottie Splendor. *(offers her hand)*

WILADINE
Dottie, this is Pearl Remington, a soon-to-be-famous novelist.

DOTTIE
What a coincidence! I'm a soon-to-be-famous news reporter!

PEARL
At WPDQ-Radio? Good luck with that. They don't hire girls except to fetch a cup of Joe.

WILADINE
Controlling the coffee pot has its perks. Besides, who needs famous? I'd settle for comfortable.

(WILADINE)
GOT MY PIECE OF PARADISE.
NOT MUCH TO BRAG ON,
BUT DANG, IT'S NICE.

(PEARL)
I GOT CREATIVE CONTROL,

(DOTTIE)
I WAS ON A BAD ROLL,

(ALL THREE)
WHEN A NEW VISION CAME ALONG.

(WILADINE & PEARL)
NOW I'M HANGIN' ON--

(DOTTIE)
AND IT'S NOT JUST A PHASE.

(WILADINE & PEARL)
WE'RE HANGIN' ON,

(DOTTIE)
GIRLS GET JOBS NOWADAYS.

        (WOMEN)
        IT'S FOR CERTAIN MEN ARE
        LEARNIN'
        WE'RE DESERVIN' AND
        DETERMINED
        TO KEEP EARNIN' FROM RADIO
        DAZE.

MEN unfreeze and sing in spotlight from BOB'S office.

(MEN)
I'M HANGIN' ON

        AND IT'S NOT JUST A PHASE.

WE'RE HANGIN' ON--

        (DOTTIE)
        SO JUST LET ME REPHRASE.

(MEN)	(WOMEN)
IT'S FOR CERTAIN	IT'S FOR CERTAIN
WE'RE DESERVIN'	MEN ARE LEARNING
AND DETERMINED,	WE'RE DESERVIN'
SO WE'RE YEARNIN'	AND DETERMINED,
TO KEEP EARNIN'	TO KEEP EARNIN'
FROM RADIO DAZE.	FROM RADIO DAZE.

BLACKOUT

SCENE 2

*LIGHTS UP in
IRVING's office.*

IRVING
(*talking on phone*) I don't care what you think. I know, I know. You're from the network. Well, so am I. (*pause*) What do you mean my name is offensive? Irving Lipschitz...that's my name. It's offensive? Go with my middle name? Ok...my middle name is Irving. That's right, IRVING! I was named after my two grandfathers, Irving and Irving...Lipschitz and Russell.

Don't tell me! I have show business contacts. I once played golf with Vic Damone. And I had lunch with Ish Kabibble. That's right, THE Ish Kabibble!

We have your radio play. A western. Maybe THE western that'll set new standards in the industry. What's it called? Ahhh, it's called...no, I have it right here. It's called...ahhh...Ride To Toadstool, I mean Tombstone. Tombstone. Ride To Tombstone. The stars? I can't tell you right now. Because I can't, but this is a big cast with some of the biggest names in the industry. Let me put it this way. Ever heard of Clark Gable? Yeah, well, so have I. *(Motions to Dottie. She enters. A not too smart young girl very anxious to be part of all of this. Her first job. He covers the phone)* Can we get Gable on the phone?

DOTTIE
(*She smiles and looks confused*) Really! Clark Gable? Ohhhh, he's just dreamy!

IRVING
No, not Clark Gable. We can't get him. I meant Herb Gable, the old time movie star. He goes by Barrymore Johnathan Selden. Get him, if you can find him. If not...well, just get him. He may be at his club. I think he's the Maître D, or the dish washer, or something.

DOTTIE
Yes, sir! (*she exits*)

IRVING
Sorry, I had to put you on hold. Someone very important came in. Who? Ahhhh, have you ever heard of James Cagney? Well, so have I. Ok, we'll be talking soon.

DOTTIE
(enters) Barrymore isn't at his club, anymore. He's in the publishing business, now.

IRVING
Really?!

DOTTIE
Yeah, he delivers newspapers.

IRVING
Ok, great. Call him up, after he finishes his paper route, and tell him we have a job for him. But, don't give him a dollar figure. I think we can get him cheap. The only problem is, he likes to write his own dialog. He actually got a job as a writer on GONE WITH THE WIND. He lasted about three days.

DOTTIE
What happened?

IRVING
You know the line, "Frankly my dear, I don't give a damn?"

DOTTIE
Oh, yes.

IRVING
Well he wanted to change it to, "Bug off Scarlett, what are you, stupid, or something?" We need a sound man. I want the best in the business, the BEST. I sent out 5 letters to five guys who know me and that I've worked with before. I think they'll jump at the chance to get on board with us.

DOTTIE
Oh, I have the responses. I forgot. I had them clothes pinned to the fan on my desk. It makes it sound like a motor-scooter!

IRVING
Fine. Just read the responses. Start with Teddy Thompson. He's the one I want. If he's busy, we'll work our way down the list. Old Teddy...he loves me. *(she opens letter)* I remember when he needed the sound effect of a gate opening in a rain storm. He said, "Who opens a gate in a....." What's wrong?

              DOTTIE
Well...he says...

              IRVING
Old Teddy...that crazy nut. I remember the time he... What is it? You look funny.

              DOTTIE
I don't know if I should read this.

              IRVING
Old Teddy.... Go ahead, and don't hold back.

              DOTTIE
 He says, and I quote: "I remember you, Lipschitz, and I would rather eat a dead vulture than to work with you, again. I'd rather fall off the Chrysler Building than be associated with you. I can't stand you, you son of a..."

              IRVING
Yeah, I get it. Must be because of that money he thinks I owe him.

              DOTTIE
Why does he think that?

              IRVING
Because I owe him money.

              DOTTIE
There's more.

              IRVING
What else could there be?

              DOTTIE
And, I quote: "I've talked to every sound man out there. None of them will work with you, either."

              IRVING
My God! You know what that means, don't you? I'm stuck with Rob Bernstein. You know about him, don't you? He drinks.

              DOTTIE
So? A lot of people drink.

              IRVING
Not like this guy. He eats shredded wheat every morning.

DOTTIE
So? A lot of people eat shredded wheat for breakfast.

IRVING
Yeah, but instead of putting milk on it, he uses bourbon. His idea of a mixed drink is rum, vodka and gin in a large thermos. One time he was so drunk that he was supposed to have gunshots right at the end of radio western.

DOTTIE
And...

IRVING
Instead of gunshots, he had a waterfall and the opening of a coconut.

DOTTIE
So, we can't use him?

IRVING
Are you kidding? If he's available, call him up. Rob Bernstein. We have his number in the files. *(to himself, delays with business)* My God, Rob Bernstein...

DOTTIE
He's on the phone.

IRVING
Line one?

DOTTIE
There's more than one?

IRVING
Never mind, I'll take it. Rob. Robbo. My friend, Rob. How are you?

SPOT on ROB with phone

ROB
Who is this?

IRVING
It's your old buddy, your best friend, we've been tight for years. Irving Lipschitz.

ROB
I'm sorry, that name offends me.

IRVING
I'm the one has to live with it, Rob.

ROB
What do you want, I'm a busy man. I've got something really important on my mind.

IRVING
What happened, didja lose your shot glass?

ROB
That offends me. Not as much as your name, but that offends me. I don't drink anymore. I gave it up twelve years ago. So don't pull any of your old crap, I'm thinking clearly now and can smell bullhocky over the phone.

IRVING
Wow, what a talented nose. But me, I've got a nose for talent, and I need you.

ROB
Are you going to pay me this time?

IRVING
Why does everyone keep asking me that? Of course I'll pay you. I know this stock broker—

ROB
I'm not falling for that one again. I got 6000 shares of U.S. Cardboard, and will end up leaving it to the Origami Club.

IRVING
No, I'm paying cash this time. I need a sound guy, and you're the soundest guy I know. Even when you were sloshed, your effects were the best. You'll knock the socks off WPDQ-RadioDaze audience.

ROB
You're still at PDQ? I thought that went belly up.

IRVING
We're still hanging on. Don't pay attention to those rumors about television taking over. Radio will never die.

ROB
Okay. I'm in. When do you need me? And what flavor should I bring?

####### IRVING
It's a western. I'll leave the sound choices up to you, Rob. And—thanks. *(hangs up and exits)*

> *ROB enters IRVING's office.*

####### ROB
(to DOTTIE) Hi, I'm Rob Bernstein, the sound guy. Irving called me?

####### DOTTIE
How'd you get here so fast?

####### ROB
Well, it is PDQ-Radio, after all. *(she doesn't get it)* I live right around the corner.

####### DOTTIE
It's a pleasure to meet you.

####### ROB
I haven't heard that in a long time.

####### DOTTIE
(pulls him aside) Mr. Bernstein . . .?

####### ROB
Call me Rob.

####### DOTTIE
Okay Rob. No offense, but you don't still drink, do you?

####### ROB
I've been on the wagon 12 years. Every day's a gift. I already explained that to Irving. Why do you ask?

####### DOTTIE
My dad's a drinker. He's been on the wagon, and fallen off more times than I can remember, and my Mom can't count on him for anything. That's why I'm here, to build a career and not have to depend on nobody…I mean anybody.

####### ROB
Hope the best for your dad, and I'm proud of your attitude. If he ever wants help or just to talk, have him call me. *(gives her his card)*.

####### DOTTIE
Gee thanks, Rob.

ROB
Everyone's got to find their own way out of that mess. *(Her face falls)* But sure, glad to help if I can. Maybe we can grab a …?

DOTTIE
Let me show you to the sound studio. *(exits)*

ROB
…cup of coffee later? Or dinner? A movie? *(follows her out)*

BLACKOUT

SCENE 3

Lights up in BOB's office. PEDRO wears distinctively-colored wig.

BOB
What can I do for you, Miss…?

PEDRO
Pepper. I'm Pedro Pepper, one of the popular Peppers, performing punctually at the Pink Parakeet. You owe me money.

BOB
What?

PEDRO
Pepper. I'm Pedro Pepper, one of the popular Peppers, performing punctually at …

BOB
…at the Pink Parakeet. I don't owe you money.

PEDRO
I'm positive you owe the Pepper Sisters money.

BOB
Where were you performing prior to the Pink Parakeet.

PEDRO
Pongo Pongo Club.

BOB
Oh, that's Patty Poster's place?

PEDRO
Perhaps.

BOB
How can I owe the Pepper Sisters money?

PEDRO
We sang popular presentations for WPDQ last fall. Our voices sing your call letters.

AUDIO CUE of WPDQ Jingle. PEDRO sings along.

BOB
That's you? How do you sing such pretty parts so perkily?

PEDRO
Practice. Now our latest promotion at Niagra Falls requires pesos to produce.

BOB
How much?

PEDRO
Plenty. Probably $675. And your part owed the Pepper Sisters is $75. So pay!

BOB
That's a problem. This Podunk place has few pesos, but our station manager gives great stock tips. I'll get back to you pronto.

PEDRO exits, and PEARL enters

BOB
I know you're wondering why I called you here.

PEARL
Mom said it was important. Of course, everything's important to mom. Except my novel.

BOB
Forget about novel pipe dreams. What was your novel about again?

PEARL
It's gonna be great. It's about a sailor named Buck Rowdy on a torpedo boat. What he really wants to be is a rodeo rider.

BOB
Writer? Like you? What a loser… Well anyway.

PEARL
What do you want, Uncle Bob. Buck Rowdy is a-calling me. When the muse calls, I gotta listen…

BOB
You may not have noticed, Pearl, but your Uncle Bob's dream – this radio station – has seen better days.

PEARL
(tasting coffee and making a face) I guess that explains the coffee grounds in the old sock.

BOB
Adds flavor. And you can use it over and over – but I digress.

PEARL
Sorry about the station. What else concerns you?

BOB
I'm using two-year-old weather reports, our advertisers are dropping off like full ticks from a dog.

PEARL
Ew. Hey, can I use that? *(scribbles notes)*

BOB
We haven't had a real star in here since Jimmy Stewart. And he just stopped to asked directions.

PEARL
Why am I here?

BOB
Can you keep a secret?

PEARL
No. Well, yes, but it'll cost you. Mom gives me two bucks a week to keep her up to date on everything. Give me $3 bucks and . . .

BOB
I can give you $1.50 and owe you the rest.

PEARL
(makes a note on pad) Okay, sign this.

BOB
Don't you trust me?

PEARL
I know you, Uncle Bob.

BOB
You're the type person would give your book away for free, but charge $5 a pop for an autograph.

PEARL
(dreamily) Someday…

BOB
You don't understand. I'm really hurt.

PEARL
Is it your bunions? Your rheumatism? Hemorrhoids? Gout? Did your breakfast back up on you this morning? I told you Mom tells me everything. She talks in her sleep. *(taking notes, to herself)* This is great material!

BOB
No, it's the station, don't you understand? It's WPDQ.

PEARL
What does that have to do with me?

BOB
You pretend to be writer.

PEARL
Really? And you pretend to own a radio station. *(starts to leave)*

BOB
Wait. I need you to write for the station.

PEARL
Write what? A script? About Buck Rowdy? (*starting to get excited*)

BOB
I don't care what you write, as long as it brings in some new advertisers.

PEARL
You want songs? Buck Rowdy is a great singer. I know a song writer can help us out.

BOB
Who?

PEARL
Ever heard of Johnny Mercer?

BOB
You can get Johnny Mercer?

PEARL
I can even get Bob Hope. Wait a minute, did I say Johnny Mercer? I meant Donny Mercer. He's my yard guy and works for donuts.

BOB
Works for doughnuts? That means he works cheap?

PEARL
No, that's the name of the place he works. Doughnuts. What's in this for me? Better be more than a $1.50 and an IOU.

BOB
I know my sister's demanding. It's got to be hard to find time to concentrate on your Great American Novel.

PEARL
Demanding? How would you like to rub lotion on your mother's feet twice a night?

BOB
I've seen her feet. She makes bunions look good. Here's what I can do for you, Pearl. Did I ever tell you you're my favorite niece?

PEARL
I'm your only niece. So again, what's in it for me?

BOB
What would you say to a summer on the coast, with nothing to do but dip your toes in the surf and scribble your Rowdy novel?

PEARL
Sounds like a dream. I didn't know you had a place like that.

BOB
I don't. But I've got a friend of a friend, who knows a guy's cousin, who has a place just like that. I've seen postal cards.

PEARL
So, I just write you a radio play, and you'll fund my summer getaway?

BOB
Is it a deal? It's gotta be good, Pearl

PEARL
(*clears throat, sings a capella*)
HE ROAD INTO TOWN AND HIS NAME WAS BUCK
HE ROAD A HORSE, CUZ HE DIDN'T HAVE A TRUCK
TRUCKS WOULDN'T BE INVENTED FOR ANOTHER 40 YEARS
SO HE DIDN'T HAVE TO WORRY 'BOUT SHIFTING GEARS.
BUCK, OH BUCK, HE'S BUCK, YESSSERREE THAT'S BUCK
YIPEE-YIPPEE-YEEHAW, THAT'S BUCK. (WHIP-CRACK)

BOB
Now THAT'S a western song!

They shake hands, each holds fingers crossed behind their backs.

PEARL & BOB
(*under breath, TOGETHER*) Sucker. (BOB exits. PEARL sings in SPOTLIGHT)

HUNTING FOR MY MUSE

IT'S A TALE THAT'S CAUTIONARY,
THAT CAN HAPPEN TO UNWARY
BUT WHEN YOU'RE LITERARY,
THERE'S NO CHOICE.

IT'S BEYOND THE ORDINARY
AND CAN BE A LITTLE SCARY,
WHEN YOU PICK A LI-BA-RARY
FOR YOUR MATE.

WRITING, I'M FIGHTING,
I'M HUNTING FOR MY MUSE.
SUPPOSING, COMPOSING,
DON'T WANT TO CONFUSE.

> *instrumental break, PEARL ends in IRVING's office.*

NEVER CHOSE A MONASTERY,
BUT MY WORK BECOMES PRIMARY
A LIFE THAT'S LUMINARY,
THAT'S MY FATE.

MY BEST FRIEND'S A DICTIONARY,
SO I NEED SOME MONETARY,
LONG BEFORE OBITUARY
TAKES MY VOICE.

FICTION, TAKES DICTION,
PATTER CAN AMUSE,
EQUIPTING, FOR SCRIPTING
AND THAT PAYS MY DUES.

BESIDES—I GOT NOTHIN' TO LOSE.

> *SPOT off, lights up IRVING's office, as WILADINE enters.*

SCENE 4

WILADINE
Pearl, your Uncle Bob is more excited than I've seen him in years. *(hugs her)* So glad you took him up on his offer!

PEARL
Shhh, don't tell anyone he's my uncle. How do you know everything, anyway?

WILADINE
Nobody notices the cleaning lady. I might as well be the lamp.

PEARL
You're the cleaning lady now? That's just not right!

WILADINE
No, honey, I asked for the job. That $26 a week didn't stretch far enough. And after the cleaning crew quit, Bob – I mean, the boss – gave me an extra $5 to sweep up. *(dreamy)* I'd do anything for him. I mean, for WPDQ.

> *DOTTIE enters, listening*

PEARL
I remember when you babysat for me and the other kids. I thought you were the bee's knees.

WILADINE
Always thought you were mighty special. It was like I finally had my own kids, sharing the swing shift with your mom and the other ladies at the factory, and singing along with WPDQ radio while riveting.

> *AUDIO CUE, sing WPDQ jingle*

PEARL
When Dad came home from the war, and Mom came home from the factory, we missed seeing you.

WILADINE
Hard times. Nothing paid like the factory job. *(brightens)* But your mom put in a word for me, and that's how I got this job. Been here going on 5 years, and feels like home.

DOTTIE
Gee wilikers, Wiladine, I never knew that about you. You're the glue that holds this whole station together. Maybe someday I can make $26 a week doing what you do.

WILADINE
No, don't settle for being a Girl Friday. You need to specialize, honey, find your calling and go after it with guns blazing. *(PEARL and WILADINE exit)*

DOTTIE
If ladies can rivet airplanes, I know I can nail news stories, too. Hey, Benny, can I talk to you?

> *LIGHTS UP studio & BENNY office area. Wit ROB on platform above. He brightens when DOTTIE enters. She ignores him, so he eavesdrops and interjects inappropriate sound effects.*

BENNY
You get paid to just stand around all day?

ROB
(*rude sound*) Sorry, I'm practicing. Don't let me bother you. No really, please, carry on. (*another rude sound*).

DOTTIE
I don't get paid at all. I'm working to build my re-soooom.

BENNY
Do you mean resume?

DOTTIE
What's that?

BENNY
You know, a list of all the jobs you've done. That's important. To get you the next step up in your career.

DOTTIE
Yeah, that! I want your job. Teach me how?

ROB
(*evil laugh sound*)

BENNY
You want me to train you to take over my news job? Unbelievable. Here's what you need to do, here's your first lesson. (*He molds her face into exercises he does, speaks under his breath as he exits*) That'll keep her busy for an hour.

DOTTIE
(*Stands there, manipulating face*) Gee, what a nice man!

Lights fade in studio, Lights up in IRVING's office.

SCENE 5

IRVING
(*yells from his office*) Hey Dottie, I need you in here quick. I need that girl group. The Pepper Sisters.

DOTTIE
(*rushes from BENNY's office, still practicing faces*) Patty, Polly, Pansy, and Pedro Pepper? I always wondered why she was named Pedro. Did her dad want a boy?

IRVING
No. He just couldn't spell Pedrofina. (*looks at her*) What's wrong with your face? Got a toothache or something? Never mind, get me their agent. They haven't worked with us for a while, but I know he'll send them back. He loved me!

DOTTIE
What's not to love? You're the best in the biz.

IRVING
(*preening*) Yes, me and Roy Rogerstein go way back. The guy loved me. There's nothing he wouldn't do for me. (*to DOTTIE*) Learn from the master.

DOTTIE
(*puzzled look*)

IRVING
Me! Learn from ME. If you want to make it in radio, it's all about relationships.

DOTTIE
Yes sir! (*exits*)

IRVING
(*to himself*) Old Roy. That crazy nut. I remember the time he talked about going over Niagra Falls in a barrel. That's Roy, for you. I tell ya, we were tight ….

DOTTIE
(*enters*) He's on the phone now.

IRVING
Line one?

DOTTIE
We don't have lines anymore. It's just a phone.

IRVING
Oh, I forgot. The owner's cutting cost every nit-picky way he can. That Bob Hope sure is a penny pincher. (*answers phone*) Hey Roy! What are the chances of getting that girl quartet back? Oh, it's a trio now? Really! Which one. Pedro, huh. She's dead. How did it happen? Really? Niagra

Falls in a barrel. Hell yes, I'm going to pay them. Don't I always? Well, last time I gave them something better than money. That's right. Cardboard futures! Not my fault if they can't take advantage of a good stock tip.

> *DOTTIE eavesdrops, writes down stock tip.*

IRVING
This time, I've got something even better. *(almost whispering into phone)* Keep this under your hat. You ready? Mining stock. Zinc is going to be the next big thing. Shhhh, don't tell anyone. There, I paid you in advance. *(long pause)* What in the hell do you mean, you won't send the girls over? Look, I bent over backwards for you, Roy. Okay, it's your loss. And you can tell the girl quartet that it's their loss, too. Oh that's right, I forgot about Pedro. Niagra Falls in a barrel, huh? I'm hanging up, our 30-year friendship is over. I don't want any more contact with you. Hello? Hello? How about that? He hung up on me. *(aside)* Where am I'm going to get a girl trio?

> *WILADINE enters dusting, humming and singing.*

IRVING
(to DOTTIE) Do you hear what I hear?

DOTTIE
(sings) "A star, a star, brighter than the …"

IRVING
No, not the Christmas carol. *(whispers)* Her.

DOTTIE
Oh.

IRVING
We need a girl trio. Make it happen. *(exits)*

DOTTIE
Hi Wiladine. Did you ever think about being a professional singer?

WILADINE
That's always been my dream. But working here at WPDQ is the closest I've come to show biz. By the way, there's a lady waiting in the green room.

DOTTIE
Oh, she must be here for the weekend receptionist job. I'll be right back, don't go anywhere. I need to talk to you. *(exits, quickly reenters with ROSIE)* So do you type?

ROSIE
Not really.

DOTTIE
Take shorthand?

ROSIE
Why do you ask?

DOTTIE
You do know how to answer the phone, right?

ROSIE
Of course. When do I meet the owner, Bob Hope? I understood my appointment was with him.

WILADINE
(*under her breath*) Bob Hope. He's dreamy…

DOTTIE
Oh, nobody talks to Mr. Hope. He's super busy. And my boss, Mr. Lipschitz, gave me the authority to hire. So – welcome to …

AUDIO CUE, All sing WPDQ jingle.

ROSIE
Hey, we're good!

DOTTIE
By the way, what's your name? If you're going to work here we need to know what to call you. I'm Dottie and this is Wiladine.

ROSIE
Rosalind P. Walter. But I go by Rosie, ever since working the night shift riveting the F4U Corsair fighter planes. You mean, I got the job? What exactly do you expect me to do?

DOTTIE
You'll catch on real quick. We're a family here at WPDQ. Part of your job involves filling in. As needed. You know, answering the phone, making

appointments, fetching coffee. Making nice with the sponsors. Singing here and there.

ROSIE

Here and there?

DOTTIE

As needed.

PROJECTION of named products as the song is performed. Each actor touts her own favorite sponsor products, sung almost as an "I can top yout" challenge.

SPONSORS

(WILADINE)
ORANGE CRUSH AND DIXIE CUPS,
TONI AT-HOME PERMANENTS,
TOWN TALK BREAD AND BRECK SHAMPOO,
MANOR HOUSE AT 50 CENTS.

(DOTTIE)
AVON LADIES, CHESTERFIELDS,
EVENING IN PA-REE PERFUME.
BURMA-SHAVE AND UNCLE SAM
IPANA TOOTHPASTE, I PRESUME.

(ROSIE)
PAPER DOLLS, ERECTOR SETS,
TINKER TOYS AND LINCOLN LOGS,
IVORY SOAP AND BETSY WETS.
SEARS & ROEBUCK CATALOGS.

PEARL joins WILADINE in IRVING's office, DOTTIE escorts ROSIE to BOB's office, DOTTIE joins BENNY in his office. The three pairs continue singing their verses, repeating 4 times, miming radio business conversations.

(WILA. & PEARL)
ORANGE CRUSH
AND DIXIE CUPS
TONI AT-HOME
PERMANENTS,
TOWN TALK
BREAD & BRECK
SHAMPOO,
MANOR HOUSE AT
50 CENTS.

(DOTTIE & BENNY)
AVON LADIES,
CHESTERFIELDS
EVENING IN PARIS
PERFUME.
BURMA-SHAVE &
UNCLE SAM,
IPANA
TOOTHPASTE, I
PRESUME.

(ROSIE & BOB)
PAPER DOLLS,
ERECTOR SETS,
TINKER TOYS AND
LINCOLN LOGS,
IVORY SOAP AND
BETSY WETS.
SEARS&ROEBUCK
CATALOGS.

BLACKOUT

SCENE 6

PROJECTION of outside WPDQ building, played in SPOTLIGHT.

BOB
Pedro Pepper! Don't procrastinate on that stock tip, potent paper brings positive returns!

PATTY
(Wears different color wig than before) Pedro died. I'm Patty Pepper. And you still owe the Pepper Sisters money.

BOB
That Niagra Falls promotion?

PATTY
Was supposed to be a barrel of laughs.

BOB
Too bad, when promotions wash out like that.

PATTY
You can say that again. Where's the money you owe us?

BOB
I'll go check with my stock guy. He's over here. (*He points one way, rushes the other direction, leaving her frustrated.*)

SCENE 7

LIGHTS UP in Greenroom

SNAZZY
My God, I know you! Barrymore Jonathan Seldon. You used to be in pictures, you use to be big!

BARRY
I'm still big. Just the pictures got small.

SNAZZY
Pleased ta meetcha, call me Snazzy. I'm in pictures, too. Well, in radio, and soon in television. That's the next big thing, you know.

BARRY
Television can never match the majesty of the theater, the dynamics of the silver screen, a 40-foot image that has cast a spell over an entire audience. The spectacle of the talking picture.

SNAZZY
Wow. That's beautiful. What are you doing these days?

BARRY
I was in paper products until cardboard futures went bust. Now I sell shoe polish. It doubles as hair tonic. Comes in 17 shades. Cordovan is my best seller.

SNAZZY
I guess you wonder what I'm doing here.

BARRY
No, not really.

SNAZZY
I'm the new sales guy for WPDQ. Well, I'm interviewing, but I'm a shoe–in.

BARRY
That's my line. And I got the polish for you! Wait a minute. I'm interviewing for that job, too.

SNAZZY
Name it, and I can sell it. Go ahead, give me a challenge. I dare you, I double dog dare you. I need this job, and nobody's getting my spot. I even write my own ad copy. There's nothing too small or too big that I can't make 'em beg to buy from me.

SNAZZY MALONEY

(SNAZZY)
HEY, I'M SNAZZY MALONEY.

(BARRY)
YOU ARE FULL OF BALONEY.

(SNAZZY)
I CAN SELL ANYTHING AT ALL.
WASHERS, DETERGENT, WHISTLES, AND CARS,
JUST GO ON AND GIVE ME A CALL.

(BARRY)
IT'LL COST ME TOO MUCH.

(SNAZZY)
NO, I'LL BARGAIN AND SUCH.
YOU'LL LOVE WHAT I SELL, HAVE NO FEARS.
LOLLIPOP CANDY, DRESSES, AND BROOMS,
BEEN SELLING STUFF FOR LOTS OF YEARS.

(music break 14 measures)

SNAZZY
I'll bet you dollars to doughnuts that I can sell a bigger, better, high-dollar ad faster than you can!

BARRY
I'll take that bet!

> *They shake hands, look around for prospects and end up singing and "selling" to the audience.*

(SNAZZY)
HOW 'BOUT A DEAL!

          (BARRY)
          IS THIS GUY FOR REAL?

MY ORDER BOOK IS FULL
OF MY WARES.
RADIOS, GIRDLES, GLOVES
AND SKATES,
TICKETS TO THE
COUNTY FAIRS.

          SELLING'S MY LIFE.

JUST ASK HIS EX-WIFE.

          I POLISH EV-ER-Y ROLE.
          COMEDY, DRAMA,
          MOVIES AND SONGS,

SO SHINING SHOES
IS SAVING YOUR SOLES?

PEARL enters, both try to sell to her.

(BOTH)
YOU NEED WHAT I SELL,

(SNAZZY)
GOT IPANA AND PRELL.

(BARRY)
THIS GUY'S GOT A LOT OF BRASS!

(SNAZZY)
VICEROY, LUCKIES, CHESTERFIELD SMOKES.

(BOTH)
GOT ORDERS CLEAR UP TO MY ASS-ETS.

          PEARL
Quit hounding me. I'll have the radio script ready soon!

          SNAZZY
Hmnn. WPDQ acquiring a new radio script? Sales alert! They'll need sponsors for that!

          BARRY
Script? Young woman, there is a script, you say? Perhaps a part for a young, dashing hero? *(he poses).*

PEARL
Wait. I know you! You're that famous . . . *(he poses again)* shoe polish guy, Barrymore Johnathan Seldon. My mom loves your bunion lotion.

BARRY
I'm incognito. I'm merely doing research for a part. But I have been known to perform for select, discriminating audiences. So . . . this script of yours, I'm sure we could come to an understanding? I'd love to elevate your work to the heights, promote it to the skies, shine it to the high, patent-leather gloss it deserves. (*BARRY and PEARL huddle*)

DOTTIE
(enters) Mr. Maloney? The station owner, Mr. Hope, says he can see you now. Walk this way. *(walks very distinctively. SNAZZY mimics her walk as they exit, leaving BARRY to sing, SPOTLIGHT)*

KINDA

BACK IN THOSE DAYS I WAS ABLE,
AS BIG AS TRACY OR GABLE.
BROUGHT MY A-GAME TO THE TABLE,
KINDA. KINDA.

LADIES SWOONED WHEN I PLAYED THE LOVER,
AROUND MY DRESSING-ROOM THEY'D HOVER.
SOMETIMES I'D HAVE TO RUN FOR COVER.
KINDA. KINDA.

(spoken to PEARL) But what the hell happened? Well I'll tell you.

STARTED IN SILENTS
CAM'RA LOVED ME
COULD DO NO WRONG
IN MY CAREER, YOU SEE.
ON SCREEN WITH GARBO
AND PICKFORD, TOO.
HELD MY OWN,
EVEN KISSED A FEW.
THEN SOUND CAME IN,
AND THEY LOVED MY VOICE.
COULD HAVE RETIRED,
YES, I HAD THE CHOICE.
DECIDED TO STAY,
HAD TO PERSEVERE.
NOTHING TO LOSE,
I HAD NOTHING TO FEAR.

(*spoken*) Then I was fired.

WANDERED AROUND
FOR LOTS OF YEARS.
STOKING MY EGO,
SHEDDING LOTS OF TEARS.
GOT TIRED OF HEARING,
"DON'T I KNOW YOU?"
HAPPENED A LOT OF TIMES,
NOT JUST A FEW.

I WANNA GO BACK
I REALLY DO.
I WANNA SHARE
A LINE OR TWO THAT'S NEW.
I'LL GET BACK IN,
JUST YOU WAIT AND SEE,
I'LL WORK FOR CASH.
YES, I'LL WORK FOR FREE.

PEARL
Well, I'll see what I can do. (*exits*)

NOW SELLING POLISH TO THE MASSES,
AND SALES ARE SLOW AS MOLASSES.
GOSH, I WAS BIG WITH THE LASSES.
KINDA. KINDA.

DIZZY *enters and watches.*

HEADED RIGHT BACK TO THE BIG TIME REAL SOON.
AND ONCE AGAIN ALL OF THE FANS WILL SWOON.
I'LL HAVE THEM HOWLING AGAIN AT THE MOON.
KINDA. KINDA.

(*spoken to audience*) Wanna buy some shoe polish? (*SPOT off*)

DIZZY
What the hell are you doing here?

BARRY
(*shocked*) Desdemona Norman! (*gathers composure*) What am I doing here? What am I doing here? Question is, what are YOU doing here, my fair woman?

DIZZY
Cut the crap. That didn't work when we were married, and it won't work now. Shoe polish? Really? Oh, how the mighty are fallen.

BARRY
There's a reason everyone calls you Dizzy. Our marriage was the worse 16 years of my life.

DIZZY
We finally agree on something. Except it was 16 months.

BARRY
When you're in hell, time runs like dog years. Every day felt like a decade.

DIZZY
So how is Wolfie these days? Still 200 pounds of slobbering fur?

BARRY
That was 25 years ago. And he's doing great. I see you're still trying to look like your headshot.

DIZZY
So are you, but with you it's not working. Might try some of that brownish stuff on your head.

BARRY
Ha ha. Shows how much you know. It's Cordovan.

DIZZY
My gosh, you're actually using that stuff? Sad times, Barry, sad times.

BARRY
I heard your career's going great. Last month, a fan letter poured in.

DIZZY
Mordy got me this gig. He's always working the angles, you wisenheimer, so just you wait. But why are you even here? Your career went sideways long ago. I thought you were delivering newspapers. Are you the new Boot Black spokesman?

BARRY
I'm merely incognito. I'm researching a role for a possible play that I'm producing.

DIZZY
Death of a Shoe Polish Salesman?

                    BARRY
You've heard of it?

                    DIZZY
Go with your strengths, Barry. Give 'em the performance audiences have come to expect. Hey, it's great reminiscing but I gotta find the director of this dump.

                    BARRY
Lipschitz.

                    DIZZY
How dare you!

                    BARRY
No, that's his name. Irving Irving Lipschitz. But I got here first.

                    DIZZY
Ladies first, Barry. *(crosses to IRVING's office)*

                    BARRY
Sure, Dizzy. I always did come in last with you.

BLACKOUT

Scene 8

Lights up in IRVING's office.

                    DOTTIE
(looking over shoulder) There's a woman outside, says she's got a bone to pick with you.
                    IRVING
I didn't do it!

                    DOTTIE
Do what?

                    IRVING
Whatever it is, it wasn't me. It was . . .

DIZZY
(sweeps into room, glamorous) Are you the guy in charge?

IRVING
My God, you're Desdemona Norman. I'd know that voice anywhere! I saw all your movies. Warbling In The Drizzle, Gone With The Gust, Meet Me In St. Paul, Guys & Gals. What d'ya know, old Mordy came through for me.

DIZZY
(preening) And you are…?

IRVING
Oh, sorry. *(offers his hand, she ignores it)* Irving Lipschitz, I'm the director. *(offers her a chair, she takes it. To DOTTIE)* This is THE Desdemona Norman. The Dizzy Girl everyone loves!

DOTTIE
(awed, but not a clue who she is). I guess you're really famous, from the olden days, huh? I always wanted to be famous someday.

DIZZY
(looks her up and down) Good luck with that, honey. *(to IRVING)* I need to make a call. Do you mind?

IRVING
Not at all. *(DIZZY takes phone, waits to dial, looks pointedly at DOTTIE until IRVING shoos her from room.)*

DIZZY
(emphatic, to IRVING) Do—you—MIND?!

IRVING takes hint and exits

DIZZY
(on phone, angry) Connect me with Mordecai Waltman. Tell him it's Desdemona Norman. Yes, it's me. Again. No, I don't want to talk to his secretary. Yes, I know he's the head guy. Hey, I'm busy too! Listen, honey, he already promised to get back to me three times this week. I don't care if he told you to hold all calls, that doesn't apply to me. He's my agent, I'm his top client, so technically he works for me. Put him on the phone.

(waits a beat, checking appearance in hand mirror as if he could see her over the phone) Mordy! What's the deal, booking me into another 3rd rate radio gig? Yeah, sorry about interrupting your meeting *(rolls eyes)*. Okay, sure, I know a job's a job. But my fans miss me! Singing gigs on has-been

radio shows isn't my idea of maintaining a career. What happened to that part on the television show, I'm still waiting for my audition slot.

(more angry as she listens). What do you mean, I'm too old? They actually said that? How dare they! *(sarcastic)* Yes, I know the part called for a 25-year-old perky flirty wifey. I can be perky. I can be flirty. I can be 25…with the right makeup and wardrobe. I'm still the DIZZY GIRL everyone loves, dammit! Hell, I've been married four times, so I've got the wifey bit down pat. I didn't even get a screen test. Doesn't experience count for anything anymore? Don't they know who I am?

> *PEARL enters, overhears*

Get me on television! Just once, and my fans will demand more. Mordy, you're top in the biz, because of me. You've still got pull. So get me my shot, you owe me that much. Yes, I know radio gave me my career, and got me my first movie. But radio's dying. Times change. *(listens)* You could do that? *(grins)* Yeah, in that case, I'll put up with this Podunk radio stuff. Just make sure it's **sooner rather than later**, Mordy. *(hangs up, doesn't sees PEARL)*

> *PROJECTION during song of famous performers named in lyrics as DIZZY sings in SPOT.*

FAMOUS

HEAD FULL OF DREAMS, HEART FULL OF HOPE
CRAZY-SMART SCHEMES . . . KNEW I COULD COPE.
"I'LL BE FAMOUS," I SWORE, THIS IS HOW IT BEGAN,
WHEN THEY OPENED THE DOOR,I HAD A GREAT PLAN.

I WALTZED WITH ASTAIRE,
DUETING WITH BING,
GIDDY-UP'D WITH JOHN WAYNE, AND
GAVE BACK GABLE'S RING.

OUT-BLINKED BETTY DAVIS,
OUT-GLAM'D HEDDY'S GROOVE,
WITH TALENT OUTRAGEOUS,
UPSTAGED GINGER'S MOVES.

MY WARBLING MORE PURE
THAN STAFFORD OR PAGE,
MY FIGURE'S ALLURE
LEFT JANE RUSSELL ENRAGED.

TURNED DOWN VINCENT PRICE,
SPENCER TRACY, AND GRANT,
WILLIAM HOLDEN WAS NICE,
GREG'RY PECK MADE ME PANT!

I GOT ALL I ASKED FOR,
BEING FAMOUS BACK THEN,
CUZ THEY COULDN'T IGNORE,
MY PERFORMANCE COMMAND.
BUT YEARS FLY TOO FAST,
AND I FEEL LIKE A WRESTLER
HANGING ON TO THE PAST,
LOOKING LIKE MARIE DRESSLER.

WHEN DANCE MOVES GET CREAKY,
AND BRIGHT EYES TO BAG,
THE YEARS BECOME SNEAKY
MY CABOOSE SEEMS TO SAG.
MY PHONE CALLS IGNORED,
AND NOBODY WILL HIRE.
GOTTA GET ME ON BOARD
AND NEW PROSPECTS ASPIRE.

I'VE BEEN FAMOUS BEFORE, I'LL BE FAMOUS AGAIN,
WHEN THEY OPEN THE DOOR, I'LL HAVE A NEW PLAN.

I'VE BEEN FAMOUS BEFORE, I'LL BE FAMOUS AGAIN.
AUDACIOUS! OUTRAGEOUS, NOT SO AIMLESS.

COURAGEOUS, OFF HIATUS, BACK ON TOP.
FINALLY FAMOUS. I WON'T STOP,
TILL I'M FINALLY FAMOUS …AGAIN!

PEARL
You're Dizzy Norman! Wow, Bob said I'd work with stars, but I never imagined. I'm Pearl Remington. *(holds out hand, DIZZY ignores it)*. Anyway, I got arm twisted to write scripts for the station.

DIZZY
(dismissive) How nice for you.

PEARL
Listen, sister, looks like we're both slumming. You'd rather be on television—and, sounds like you've got a deal cooking—and I'm just two scripts away from getting a paid year off to write my novel. Why not work

together, so we both get what we want. ***Sooner rather than later***? (*holds out hand again, and this time DIZZY takes it.*)

BLACKOUT

SCENE 9

> *LIGHTS UP BENNY at makeshift desk with typewriter, reading his prepared script. On soundstage platform above, ROB messes with sound effects.*

BENNY
(*practicing, vocalizing/warm up for news stories, spray throat, awful voice*) To be or not to be . . . (*clears throat, and makes notes on a paper on the desk*). Headlining the news today, Fern Wilkensen has reported three of her best laying hens stolen. Fern says, and I quote, "Someone took them layers, leavin' me with egg all over my face. I hate a thief, and a chicken thief is the worst. If you're out there, chicken thief, I'm a-comin' for ya." This reporter warned her that assault and battery with a frying pan could get her 30 days. Let's hope that Fern finds those fryers fast.

ROB
(*chickens clucking sound. BENNY glares*). Just trying to make your boring news more exciting. Sound effects are the punctuation marks of radio.

> *PEARL enters, watching*

BENNY
In other news, Abigail Abercrombie continues to improve in the local hospital after suffering smoke inhalation. She refuses to give up her smokes, though, and says (and I quote), "I'd rather fight, than switch."

ROB
(*coughing/wheezing sound*)

BENNY
And now a word from our sponsor. *(sees PEARL)*. Do you mind? I'm rehearsing here.

PEARL
Aren't you Benny Kornblat? I cannot believe you're still here! Your show was a national radio broadcast! I'll never forget what you said when the Hindenberg blew up. Everyone remembers, "Oh the humanity!" But you said,

BENNY
(talking to her) Boy, that's a lot of hot air.

PEARL
Yes, you said it just like that! I've got chills.

BENNY
The worst part about that tragedy, my car was parked right below that damn blimp. I loved that car. Now, what do you want, girly? I'm busy uncovering the news of the day.

PEARL
I need your Underwood.

BENNY
Well, I don't like to brag but…junior here--

PEARL
Your typewriter. I've got a script to finish.

BENNY
We're both writers. Only I write real life, and you write crap.

PEARL
Fiction reflects real life, don't give me that holier than thou schmaltz. Or I'll write and then kill off your character. *(to herself)* I need some kind of poignant moment to pull everything to a climax. I want the audience to laugh and cry, to tug their heartstrings.

BENNY
Did you hear my story about the stolen chickens?

PEARL
Weren't you on your way out?

BENNY
(a beat) Yes, I'm afraid so. *(wads up papers, tosses in wastebasket and exits)*

PEARL
(fishes wadded paper out of wastebasket) Hey, not bad! *(starts typing)*

SNAZZY
(*SNAZZY enters*) Hey Pearl, you're a big-time writer, I wanna try out my latest ad on you. *(clears throat and reads/chants from paper).*

COME TO BERNIE'S SHOP AND SWAP.
C'MON YOU SHOPPERS, IT'S WORTH A STOP.
BELIEVE ME WE'VE GOT JUST WHAT YOU NEED,
FROM REAL NICE RADIOS TO CHICKEN FEED.

WE'LL SEE YOU AT BERNIE'S DAY OR NIGHT.
WHERE YA GET A DEAL, AND WE DO IT RIGHT.
COME ON IN FOR A SHOPAPALOOZA,
CUZ A REAL GREAT DEAL IS WHAT WE'LL DOOZ YA!

YEAH, BERNIE'S, YEAH, BERNIE'S, YEAH, BERNIE'S.... *(fade out)*

PEARL
(*nods off during ad*)

SNAZZY
I'll take that as a maybe. *(exits)*

ROB
(*wha-wha-whaaaaaa disappointment sound*).

PEARL starts awake, and they recognize each other.

ROB & PEARL
I know you!

PEARL
We've worked together…

ROB
…before. You may not ….

BOTH
…remember me but…*(both stop and smile, speak together).* "Love In the Leaves: A Tree House Romance."

ROB
Those chirping birds, especially the woodpecker, were a real sound challenge. *(Peck…peck…peck sound effect)*

PEARL
You really have a way with heartbeats. *(pause)* You're different. Your shirt's tucked in.

ROB
Yeah, I cleaned up my act. Everything's different now, except for the sound effects, and those just got louder and noisier, just the way I like 'em. *(looks at script in typewriter)* A western, huh?

PEARL
It's not my best effort, but it pays the bills. So we'll need gun shots, hoof beats, whip cracking, saloon doors opening, gurgling of whisky being poured.

ROB
How about breaking glass? *(makes the sound)* Fist thumps in a fight? *(makes sound)* Broken chairs? *(picks up chair, starts to smash it)*

PEARL
Yes! I mean no! *(stops him from breaking chair)* That's why I liked working with you. Always thinking.

ROB
By the way, what can you tell me about Dottie Splendor?

PEARL
Dottie? Oh, you mean the new Girl Friday? Don't know much about her.

ROB
Me either, but I'd sure like to. If I could ever get her away from that news guy. She follows Benny around like a puppy with a squeaky toy.

> *BOB in his office runs to hide (exits) when he sees POLLY PEPPER enter.*

POLLY
I'm looking for Hope.

ROB
Aren't we all? Wait, you're one of the Perky Pepper Sisters! Sorry for your problems with Pedro.

PEARL
What happened to Pedro?

ROB
Niagra Falls . . . (*does sound effects going over*). Which Pepper are you?

POLLY
I'm Polly. Patty and Pansy aren't here.

ROB
Where's Patty?

POLLY
Patty married Paul Pirkle.

PEARL
And where's Pansy?

POLLY
She's married, too. Ran off with our manager.

ROB
What's his name…

PEARL
…pray tell?

POLLY
Ted.

ROB
Thank God.

PEARL
Why are you looking for Bob? *(aside to Rob)* I saw him hide when she came in.

POLLY
He owes the Pepper Sisters money. Actually, now it's just Pepper Sister, singular. I never planned on a solo career. I just wrote the music, and Pedro was a genius with lyrics. Our manager Wally tried—and failed. So I'm on my own.

PEARL
Gee, I'm sorry for your loss. Hard to write songs without lyrics, Polly.

ROB
You'd have to call them Polly's Wally-doodling… (*adds a rim-shot, both women glare*). Sorry, I couldn't resist.

PEARL
We're rehearsing my new script. We could use you. I just came up with a great lyric for my Rowdy character, but my regular music guy isn't available. He said somebody's gotta make the doughnuts. Never mind, long story. Hey, maybe you could help with the tune. Stick around, and I'll introduce you to Bob when he surfaces.

Scene 10

LIGHTS UP in studio area with old style stand mics for the rehearsal.

IRVING
Okay, I need my full cast here.

DOTTIE
We don't have a full cast.

IRVING
Who didn't show up this time?

DOTTIE
Everyone.

IRVING
Let's start mixing and matching. At least it's just a rehearsal. We've got two hours to show time. Let's make this work. Who's here?

DOTTIE
We got the shoe polish salesman. Sound effects guy. The script girl. The cleaning lady. And the front desk woman.

DIZZY
Where's my coffee I ordered?

IRVING
And her. Hey Miss Norman, we need you.

DIZZY
Of course you do.

IRVING
(*to DOTTIE*) Go round the rest of 'em up.

DOTTIE
Yee-haw.

IRVING
Perfect. It performs itself.

DIZZY
What's my motivation?

> *The rest straggle in, ROB takes place on sound effects platform.*

IRVING
This is a make or break. We're calling it RIDE TO TOMBSTONE.

PEARL
It'd be better if it was GALLOP TO THE CEMETARY.

IRVING
(*just looks at her*) Pass out the scripts.

BARRY
Remember, I like to write my own dialogue.

PEARL
(*mutters*) Train wreck waiting to happen…

IRVING
Let's start. Places.

PEARL
Wait, who's playing what?

IRVING
(*irritated*) Just pass out the damn scripts.

PEARL
(*sulking, passes out sheets*)

IRVING
Barry, you're playing Brazos, the outlaw. Dizzy, you're playing Marshall Potter.

DIZZY
That's a part for a man.

BARRY
Close enough.

PEARL
(*to ladies*) You're playing the saloon girls. And singing the ads.

WILADINE
I've always wanted to be a saloon singer.

ROB
I already talked to Pearl about the sounds you need.

IRVING
Great. Fill in with whatever you think will work.

ROB
Gotcha, kemosabe.

IRVING
Hey Benny, you're on deck for the announcer. Cue the intro.

AUDIO CUE, and EVERYONE sings the WKDP- jingle

BENNY
(*clears throat several times*). From the thrilling days of the Wild West comes RIDE TO TOMBSTONE. Back when the men were rough, and the women were men.

DIZZY/MARSHALL
(*glares*) I hear that Bad Brazos is comin' to town.

BARRY/BRAZOS
That's me!

DIZZY
(*rolls eyes*)

BENNY
Now a word from our sponsor!

SNAZZY
(looks guilty, tries to hide)

AUDIO CUE, and ALL sing the WPDQ jingle again.

IRVING
(to DOTTIE) How are the sponsor sales going?

DOTTIE
Nieeee.

IRVING
What does that mean?

DOTTIE
It's better than UH.

IRVING
So what are you telling me?

DOTTIE
Barry and Snazzy are on it but so far…What sponsors? *(shrugs)*

BENNY
All of a sudden, we hear Brazo's horse thundering into town. *(slow clip-clop)* Brazo's horse has fire in his eyes. *(anemic neigh)* Just then, Brazos enters the saloon. *(limping bootsteps)*

BARRY/BRAZOS
I'm dry as a tumbleweed in a rainstorm. Set me up, barkeep.

DIZZY
Who's playing the bartender?

IRVING
Snazzy, you got any sponsors?

SNAZZY
(looks sheepish) Everyone wants singing jingles these days. Once I set my rhymes to chimes, I'll be selling like nobody's beeswax.

IRVING
Until then, earn your pay. Read the barkeep part.

SNAZZY/BARKEEP
(*bad read, but he thinks he's great*) I know you. You're Bad Brazos. What'll ya have? We have beer and we have whiskey. Whiskey for hard drinking men. Whiskey for men tough as saddle leather. Whiskey for men who can bite a bullet in two. What'll ya have, Brazos? (*sound effects, clinking bottles etc*)

BARRY/BRAZOS
I'd like a frozen Daiquiri.

PEARL
Where the hell did that come from? You're supposed to say, I'll have a shot of red eye.

BARRY
I don't like redeye, gives me heartburn. Besides, I like to write my own dialogue. Makes it more believable.

PEARL
Unbelievable!

IRVING
Take it from the cue line

SNAZZY/BARKEEP
Men who can bite a bullet in two. What'll ya have, Brazos? (*more clinking glasses/gurgling pours*)

BARRY/BRAZOS
(*clears throat, swaggers*) Gimme a Pink Squirrel. (*everyone looks, dumbfounded*) Does a Blue Hawaii work better?

IRVING
Cut to the song already. Benny, you sing the Rowdy part. Ladies, you sing the backup.

PEARL
Wait, not Benny…

BENNY
(*looks over lyric, angry*) This looks awfully familiar, Pearl.

PEARL
You threw it away. I just recycled. And edited a little.

POLLY
(*proudly*) And I wrote the music! (*grabs guitar*)

BENNY
(still reading) You added two more verses. To my work!

IRVING
Will you sing the damn song already?

> *BOB in office, busy with paperwork, and on phone during song. POLLY strums a few chords, continues once AUDIO sounds.*

MAKE A DIFFERENCE

(BENNY/ROWDY)
AN OLD MAN CAME AND SAT BY ME,
ONE CLOUDY, DREARY DAY.
HE SAID, "SON, I WANT YOU TO HEAR ME,
AND WHAT I'VE GOT TO SAY.
I WANTED TO MAKE A DIFFERENCE
IN JUST ONE PERSON'S LIFE,
BUT I NEVER HAD A FRIEND. I NEVER TOOK A WIFE."

HIS FACE IT LOOKED LIKE LEATHER.
HIS TEETH WERE MISSING, TOO.
I COULD TELL HE HAD SOME STORIES.
MAYBE QUITE A FEW.
SAID HE WANTED TO MAKE A DIFFERENCE
IN JUST ONE PERSON'S LIFE.
BUT HE NEVER HAD A FRIEND.
HE NEVER TOOK A WIFE.

"GUESS I WAS AN OUTLAW.
THAT'S WHAT FOLKS WOULD SAY.
THAT'S WHAT EVERYONE TOLD ME,
THEY SAID IT EV'RY DAY.
BUT I WANTED TO MAKE A DIFFERENCE
IN JUST ONE PERSON'S LIFE.
WISH I'D HAD A FRIEND.
WISH I'D HAD A WIFE."

I THOUGHT I SAW A TEAR
RUNNING DOWN HIS SUNBAKED FACE.
I COULD TELL HIS STORY HIT HARD.
I KNEW IT WAS THE CASE.   (*add girls)
HE JUST WANTED TO MAKE A DIFFERENCE   AH-OOOH
*IN JUST ONE PERSON'S LIFE.

ALL HE WANTED WAS A FRIEND.
ALL HE WANTED WAS A WIFE.

BOUGHT MYSELF A PAPER
JUST THE OTHER DAY.
I SAW THAT THE OLD MAN DIED,
AND I HAD TO LOOK AWAY.
*HE'D WANTED TO MAKE A DIFFERENCE   (*add girls)
*IN JUST ONE PERSON'S LIFE.
HE NEVER REALLY HAD A FRIEND.
HE NEVER HAD A WIFE.

I WENT TO THE OLD MAN'S FUNERAL.
IT WAS SOMETHING I HAD TO DO.
AND I SAW AN OLD WOMAN WEEPING
IN A DISTANT PEW.
*I HOPED HE'D MADE A DIFFERENCE
*IN JUST ONE PERSON'S LIFE.
BUT, THE OLD MAN DIED ALONE.
HE NEVER HAD A WIFE.

BOB enters, watches.

I LEFT BUT HAD TO WONDER,
WHY THE WOMAN CAME.

(GIRLS)
"I'LL KEEP THAT TO MYSELF,
IF IT'S ALL THE SAME."

(GIRLS & BENNY/ROWDY)
YOU SEE HE MADE A DIFFERENCE
IN THIS OLD WOMAN'S LIFE.

(BENNY/ROWDY)
HE NEVER KNEW HE HAD A FRIEND.

(GIRLS)
"I WOULD HAVE BEEN HIS WIFE."

(BENNY/ROWDY)
I VALUE THE LESSONS LEARNED
ON THAT CLOUDY, DREARY DAY.
I VALUE EV'RY BIT OF
WHAT HE HAD TO SAY.
YOU SEE, HE MADE A DIFFERENCE

IN THIS OLD WOMAN'S LIFE.
GO AND MAKE A FRIEND,
AND BE SURE TO HUG YOUR WIFE.

GO AND MAKE A DIFFERENCE
IN JUST ONE PERSON'S LIFE.
GO AND MAKE A FRIEND,
AND BE SURE TO HUG YOUR WIFE.

Moment of silence, BOB and WILADINE steal glances.

IRVING
(sees BOB, oblivious to his emotion) Great, you can play the bartender so Snazzy and Barry can go out and actually sell something.

BOB
No. I've got news.

IRVING
The ponies came in?

BOB
Shut up and listen, will ya? I've got an offer on the table from a big philanthropist interested in the future of television.

IRVING
You're selling out? Giving up the dream?

BOB
What dream? Scraping nickels and dimes with these washed up misfits?

IRVING
First TV broadcast was in 1929. It was a gimmick then, it's a gimmick now. This is 20 years later, and if it hasn't caught on by now, it never will.

BOB
Unless you've got the clams to make a counter offer, WPDQ is finished. You ever hear of R.P. Walter? His solicitor just called, and is ready to close the deal ASAP.

WILADINE
But this is a family! You don't just toss family out on their duffs after 20 years. *(refers to IRVING and BENNY)* Not without giving us a chance. Please Mr. Hope. Bob. What's the harm? Please?

IRVING
(pleading look, but doesn't want to beg)

ROSIE
I'm new here, but you've already made me feel like part of the family. If my vote counts (*meaningful pause*), what's the harm in waiting for, say, another week?

BOB
(*meets eyes with ROSIE, subtle exchange*) A week, I'll give you a week. (*exits*)

DIZZY
I'm outta here.

IRVING
You're still under contract. We got a week to save WPDQ, and you're going to help. You all are. As God is my witness…we'll never be television!

RADIO DAZE

(DIZZY)
HAD MY PIECE OF PARADISE…
HAD A LOT TO BRAG ON,
SURE WAS NICE.

(MEN)
YEARS HAVE TAKEN THEIR TOLL,
LOST CREATIVE CONTROL,

(DIZZY)
THEN TELEVISION
CAME ALONG.

(ALL but DIZZY)
NOW I'M HANGIN' ON

(DIZZY)
GIVING IN TO THE CRAZE.

(ALL but DIZZY)
JUST HANGIN' ON,

(DIZZY)
FLEXIBILITY PAYS.

(ALL)
IT'S FOR CERTAIN WE'RE DESERVIN'
AND WE PRAY OUR LUCK IS TURNIN'
TO KEEP EARNIN'
FROM RADIO DAZE.

IT'S FOR CERTAIN WE'RE DESERVIN'
AND WE PRAY OUR LUCK IS TURNIN'
TO KEEP EARNIN'
FROM RADIO DAZE.

BLACKOUT

ACT 2

BOB plays from his office while WILADINE from Irving's office, SPOT on each of them. PEARL runs back and forth between.

SCENE 1

BOB
This presents a major problem for me. For years I've wanted to get out from under this albatross of a station. At this point, there's no joy in what I do.

PEARL
Is that really how you feel?

BOB
Yes. And that's what scares me.

PEARL
Have you given any consideration to the people who work here?

BOB
No. I mean, yes. No I really haven't –well I mean, yes I have. Benny's been with me for 30 years, and he brought in Irving.

PEARL
What about Wiladine?

BOB
What about Wiladine? She's only been here what? Three years, I think. Feels like forever, though.

PEARL
Do you have any idea how much she actually does around here? WPDQ would have folded five years ago, without her plugging away. She answers the phone, books appointments, invoices sponsors, and even scrubs the damn toilets.

BOB
I never thought about that. She's my right hand man. Except she's a woman, of course.

PEARL
Hold that thought. *(crosses to WILADINE)* Have you given any thought about what to do after—I mean, when the station sells?

WILADINE
Don't you mean, IF the station sells?

PEARL
Sure, whatever, IF it sells.

WILADINE
My brother invited me to work with him. He sells Crosley Hotshots, the car of the future. Everyone wants one. *(depressed)*

PEARL
Sounds good. But what would you really like to do?

WILADINE
You mean, my dream? Well, I'd love to retire to a sweet little cabana in Cuba, with a nice fella. If I had the funds. And the cabana. And the fella. Course, all that's scarce as hen's teeth. Not that it matters, but do you know what your Uncle Bob's plans are? I mean, IF the station sells?

PEARL
That's a good question. Hold that thought. *(crosses back to BOB)* So Uncle Bob, what's your plan if the station sells?

BOB
You mean WHEN it sells? My dream is to visit a little island where life's slow, the music's hot, and the company's sweet. You know, like the song said, I never had a wife. Maybe it's too late. But I'd settle for buying a Crosley Hotshot and touring the country.

PEARL
Tour the country? By yourself? Sounds lonely.

BOB
(pause) I've spent most of my life lonely. Except when I'm here, in the middle of these crazies. Wiladine's the only one keeps the crazy to a dull roar.

PEARL

Hold that thought. *(cross to WILADINE, looks at her, starts to say something then...she's got nothing).* Hold that thought. *(returns to BOB)*

WHEN I FOUND YOU

(WILADINE)
HAS MY LIFE BEEN MISPENT, I WONDER?
WHERE DID IT DERAIL, I JUST CAN'T SAY.
I WANTED A LIFE FULL OF THUNDER!
BUT DREAMS WERE GONE IN JUST ONE DAY.

WHEN I FOUND YOU,
MY HEART BEAT FAST.
OUR FRIENDSHIP GREW.
SOMETHING TO LAST.
PLEASE NOTICE ME,
JUST ONE MORE TIME,
AND THEN WE'LL SEE
IF WE CAN RHYME.

PEARL

(returns to her) Wiladine, did you ever say anything? Did you tell him?

(BOB)
BEING HAPPY AND SUCCESSFUL, I'D LOVE.
I TRIED SO DAMN HARD, I PUSHED AND SHOVED.
WHAT HAVE I GOT NOW, YOU TELL ME!
NOT ONE HAPPY THING AS YOU CAN SEE.

WHEN I FOUND YOU,
MY HEART BEAT FAST,
OUR FRIENDSHIP GREW.
SOMETHING TO LAST.
PLEASE NOTICE ME,
JUST ONE MORE TIME.
AND THEN WE'LL SEE
IF WE CAN RHYME.

PEARL

(returns to him) Uncle Bob, it's not too late! Tell her, for heaven's sake.

(BOB & WILADINE DUET)
WHEN I FOUND YOU
MY HEART BEAT FAST,
OUR FRIENDSHIP GREW.
SOMETHING TO LAST.
PLEASE NOTICE ME,
JUST ONE MORE TIME.

Both WILADINE and BOB exit offices & slowly meet center stage.

WHEN I FOUND YOU
MY HEART BEAT FAST,
OUR FRIENDSHIP GREW.
SOMETHING TO LAST.
IF MEANT TO BE,
PLEASE HEAR MY PLEA.
AND THEN WE'LL SEE
IF YOU'LL BE MINE.

ROSIE interrupts and takes BOB back to his office, leaving WILADINE alone and bereft center stage. She returns to IRVING's office.

SCENE 2

FULL LIGHTS UP, DOTTIE and ROB at his sound stage platform.

DOTTIE
Rob, did you just see what I saw?

ROB
Susie sells sea shells by the seashore.

DOTTIE
What?

ROB
I thought it was a test. No, I only see your glowing loveliness. Wanna have coffee? Lunch? Dinner? How about …

DOTTIE
Good try, Rob, but I'm not buying.

ROB
My treat, Dottie.

DOTTIE
That Rosie isn't what she seems. First she waltzes in here for the receptionist job even before it's advertised. And then she hurts Wiladine by throwing herself at Bob. Everybody knows Wiladine is sweet on Bob.

ROB
Except for Bob.

DOTTIE
We need to get the dirt on Rosie. It's my chance to prove I can be an investigatory reporter.

ROB
It should be easy to do, too. I have a nose for things like this.

DOTTIE
Do you really?

ROB
Naw. But neither do you. Besides, girls can't be reporters. Hey, you wanna go on a picnic?

DOTTIE
If you'll help me get the dirt on Little Miss Rosier-Than-Thou, I'll go to dinner with you.

ROB
Dutch treat?

BENNY
(enters) What are you two gossiping about again?

ROB
Dottie says she's on the trail of a big news story, Benny. Watch out, she's after your job! *(sings ominous sound effect, da-da-da-dum DOOH!)*

BENNY
Oh honey, you're setting yourself up for disappointment. Stick to fetching coffee, and reading the society pages. *(tosses her the newspaper)*.

ROB
And finding a guy to take care of you.

NEWS FLASH

(BENNY & ROB)
SOME WOMEN TRIED, BUT THEY AIN'T GOT THE KNACK.

(BENNY)
I'LL LEAVE 'EM BEHIND ME WITH THE PACK.
BY THE TIME THEY SHOW UP, I'M-A COMING BACK,

(BENNY & ROB)
CUZ I'M/HE'S A NEWSMAN, JACK!

(DOTTIE)
HIPPITY HOP, I'VE GOT THE NEWS.
STRAIGHT FROM WOMAN'S POINT OF VIEWS
I NEED A PRESS PASS, AND OLD GUM SHOES
CUZ I GOT THOSE NEWSY BLUES.

DOTTIE enlists ladies in her cause, while BENNY and ROB rally the men. The song becomes an argument, men vs women: WILA vs IRVING in his office, ROSIE vs BOB in his office, etc.

GIRLS DO IT
JUST AS GOOD AS GUYS.
WHO KNEW IT!
SISTERHOOD HAS EYES.
DON'T TELL ME NO!
I'M READY TO SHOW
THE WORLD WHAT I CAN DO!

(DOTTIE, PEARL, WILADINE)	(DIZZY, POLLY, ROSIE)
HIPPITY HOP,	GIRLS DO IT
I'VE GOT THE NEWS.	JUST AS GOOD AS GUYS
STRAIGHT FROM WOMAN'S	WHO KNEW IT
POINT OF VIEWS	SISTERHOOD HAS EYES.
I NEED A PRESS PASS, AND	DON'T TELL ME NO
OLD GUM SHOES	I'M READY TO SHOW
CUZ I GOT THOSE NEWSY	THE WORLD WHAT I CAN
BLUES.	DO.

(ALL MEN)
SOME WOMEN TRIED, BUT THEY AIN'T GOT THE KNACK.
I'LL LEAVE 'EM BEHIND ME WITH THE PACK.
BY THE TIME THEY SHOW UP, I'M-A COMING BACK,
CUZ I'M A NEWSMAN, JACK!

Sung twice

(DOTTIE, PEARL, WILADINE)

HIPPITY HOP,
I'VE GOT THE NEWS.
STRAIGHT FROM WOMAN'S POINT OF VIEWS
I NEED A PRESS PASS, AND OLD GUM SHOES
CUZ I GOT THOSE NEWSY BLUES.

(ALL MEN)

SOME WOMEN TRIED, BUT THEY AIN'T GOT THE KNACK.
I'LL LEAVE 'EM BEHIND ME WITH THE PACK.
BY THE TIME THEY SHOW UP, I'M-A COMING BACK,
CUZ I'M A NEWSMAN, JACK!

(DIZZY, POLLY, ROSIE)

GIRLS DO IT JUST AS GOOD AS GUYS
WHO KNEW IT SISTERHOOD HAS EYES.
DON'T TELL ME NO
I'M READY TO SHOW
THE WORLD WHAT I CAN DO.

(ALL LADIES)
NEWS FLASH, MISTER,
CUZ THESE SISTER,
CAN DO IT
JUST AS GOOD

AS THE GUYS.

(MEN shout in rhythm)
NO WAY!

DOTTIE stalks off, ROB follows, all exits except WILADINE, POLLY and ROSIE.

SCENE 3

WILADINE
Gosh, I wasn't expecting this. What do you think?

POLLY
This is out of our league, girls. If the men in charge have lost control, how are we supposed to fix it?

ROSIE
Don't give me that drivel, honey. Men always underestimate women, and we let them. In 1949, that's how we win.

WILADINE
Boy, is that true. (*hurt, with pointed meaning*) Some women know how to win with men. Do you know how much people talk around the cleaning lady, like I'm invisible or something? I've seen everything, I've heard everything.

ROSIE
Everything? Then you know . . .

POLLY
Know what?

ROSIE
Never mind.

POLLY
When will I know?

ROSIE
In time, sweetie, in time.

WILADINE
(*shaking off the hurt*) What we need is a happily ever after. I know what mine is. And I know what Irving's is. And I guess Rosie knows what Bob's happily ever after is. I want him to be happy.

ROSIE
Fairy Godmother time?

POLLY
I'm in! Just tell me how, when, where and why to sprinkle those fairy droppings.

WILADINE
I think you mean fairy dust.

ROSIE
Uh…maybe not.

POLLY
So what's the plan? To save WPDQ?

WILADINE
We need a red-carpet premier showcasing the new and improved WPDQ. After all, what's the difference between radio and television?

ROSIE
Besides cameras? Besides money? Besides a profit?

WILADINE
No. A studio audience!

POLLY
I don't know about that. Wally, our manager, always said I got a face for radio.

WILADINE
Nuts to that. Besides, you've got a voice for television. We all do.

AUDIO CUE, sing WPDQ jingle.

With you as our lead singer, we can be the new and improved Pepper Sisters! Nobody will know the difference. The public never saw you, only heard your musical stylings. And, if WPDQ goes away, we've got a backup plan.

ROSIE
That could work. For radio and for . . . my little project.

POLLY
Don't get your hopes up, girls. Yes, success can be wonderful, but it wasn't all champagne and roses. At least not for the Pepper Sisters.

SISTERS

(POLLY)
SHOW BIZ CALLED AND WE WAS BIT.
NEVER LOOKED BACK, NOT ONCE.
MADE IT BIG IN NO TIME FLAT,
IN ONLY A FEW SHORT MONTHS.

AGENTS, BILLS, AND JEALOUSY
CAUSED MANY A SLEEPLESS NIGHT
SINGING BUSINESS LOST ITS CHARM
EACH SISTER THOUGHT SHE WAS RIGHT.

(ALL)
ONE BAD SISTER MAKES YOU BITTER,
TWO CAN MAKE YOU BLUE.
THREE TOGETHER AIN'T NO FEATHER
IN YOUR CAP.
FOUR THAT WHISPER CAUSE A BLISTER
HURTS YOU EVERYDAY.
YOU CAN'T CHOOSE, SOMETIMES YOU LOSE IT
IN A SNAP.

(POLLY)
PEDRO MET A HORRID FATE
OVER THE FALLS IN A VAT!
DIDN'T PLAN IT VERY WELL
TO LAND ON THE ROCKS IN A SPLAT.

PATTY AND PANSY TOOK IT REAL HARD
WHEN PEDRO TOOK TO THE SEA
BOTH LEFT THE BIZ ON THE ARM OF A GUY
LEAVING THE SONGS TO ME.

IF WE'D STUCK TO WRITING SONGS
IT WOULD'VE BEEN BEST FOR ALL.
PEDRO ALIVE, SISTERS SINGING OUR JIVE.
NOT BY MYSELF, FEELING SMALL.

(ALL)
ONE BAD SISTER MAKES YOU BITTER,
TWO CAN MAKE YOU BLUE.
THREE TOGETHER AIN'T NO FEATHER
IN YOUR CAP.
FOUR THAT WHISPER CAUSE A BLISTER
HURTS YOU EVERYDAY.
YOU CAN'T CHOOSE, SOMETIMES YOU LOSE IT
IN A SNAP.

(POLLY)
NO MATTER WHAT,
NO DOOR GETS SHUT
I LOVE THEM ANYWAY.

WILADINE
You can't pick family. But we can choose our singing sisters. What do you say, ladies?

BOB
What's going on in here? Coffee break's over, girls. I need my wastebasket emptied, the phone needs answering, and where's Snazzy? Has anyone sold any more sponsor spots?

(TOGETHER)
Yes sir, right away sir. (*smile and exit*)

BLACKOUT

SCENE 4

Lights Up, BENNY's desk.

PEARL
Benny, I hate to bother you, but I need your Underwood again.

BENNY
Why not? My Muse has abandoned me.

SNAZZY
Hey, glad you're both here. I got another ad for you to hear. (*clears throat and recites*)

D'YA LOOK AT A MENU AND SAY, "OK?"
CUZ IT'S GONNA BE A HEAVY EATING DAY.
STEAKS, MACARONI, TATERS WITH CHEESE.
GOES DOWN EASY, AS YOU PLEASE.

BILLY'S CAFÉ IS WHERE IT'S AT.
CHOLESTEROL, DON'T BOTHER. HEY WHAT'S THAT?
SO ROLL INTO BILLY'S, AND HIT THE DOOR.
WE EVEN HAVE A RE-ENFORCED FLOOR.

HERE AT BILLY'S WE OPEN AT NOON.
BRING YOUR APPETITE. WE'LL SEE YA SOON.
BILLY'S WAS VOTED THE VERY BEST.
IT'S GUARANTEED TO POP YOUR VEST!

PEARL
At least I didn't nod off.

BENNY
Seriously? You'd sully my reportage with that drivel? Hey, why don't you team up with that Pepper person to add punch to your poems? Even Pearl pens more proper prose.

SNAZZY
What a great idea Thanks. I'll take that as a YES! *(exits)*

PEARL
Yeah, you're damn right I write swell. Sorry about your missing muse, Benny. What's he look like?

BENNY
She. What does SHE look like. My muse is a sweet young thing who whispers sweet nothings in my ears … and lately they're next to nothing.

PEARL
Maybe your muse ran off with someone more her age. My muse is a crusty old guy who knows exactly what to say, is totally in charge, and soldiers on when everything else falls apart. But – he's not in the least romantic. I could do with some pathos.

BENNY
Pathos? *(reach in his pocket for breath mints and offers her some).* Here, I'll have one, too.

PEARL
(laughs) That's great, Benny! Can I use that?

BENNY
You mean steal it? At least you asked this time.

PEARL
Ya know, together we could write some seriously crazy-good stuff. Detective stories are very popular. Gritty crime, crusty mysteries--

BENNY
Well, I am a crusty old muse, for sure. Worth a try. *(very excited, sings to tune)* I gotta muse, you gotta muse, all God's chillum…

PEARL
Would you just stop it!

PARTNERS

(BENNY)
GREAT STEADY JOB AND ELEVATED STATUS.

(PEARL)
HEAD WRITER'S GIG! FOLKS STARING AT US.

(BOTH)
A FUTURE IN PUBLISHING, MORE STORIES TO TELL.

(BENNY)
JUST THE FACTS, JACK.

(PEARL)
HEY, MY FANTASY'S SWELL.

(BOTH)
FINISH MY SENTENCE, LOAN ME YOUR TYPEWRITER.
NO MORE REPENTENCE, ALWAYS WAS A FIGHTER.

(BENNY)
OUR FUTURE'S IN RADIO!

(PEARL)
YOU DON'T HAFTA YELL. WE'RE NOT HACKS, JACK,
BUT TV COULD SELL.

(BOTH)
FINISH MY SENTENCE, LOAN ME YOUR TYPEWRITER.
WE'LL BE RELENTLESS PULLING AN ALL NIGHTER.
WE'RE WRITING IN STERO, WHO CAN TELL.
WE'VE GOT THE KNACK, JACK! WE CAN DO WELL.

EDIT MY WRITING, HAND ME YOUR ERASER.
WE CAN'T BE FIGHTING, OR I'LL SEE YOU LATER.

(BENNY)
OUR FUTURE'S SO RADICAL!

(PEARL)
I'M UNDER YOUR SPELL. WE'LL COME BACK, JAC!
AND WE'LL DO IT WELL.

(BOTH)
FINISH MY SENTENCE, LOAN ME YOUR TYPEWRITER.
WE'LL BE RELENTLESS PULLING AN ALL NIGHTER.
WE'RE WRITING IN STEREO, WHO CAN TELL.
WE'VE GOT THE KNACK, JACK! WE CAN DO WELL.

(BENNY)
PARTNERS IN TIME,

(PEARL)
PARTNERS SUBLIME.

(BOTH)
PARTNERS IN RHYME,
HERE'S TO PARTNERS,
PARTNERS IN CRIME!

BLACKOUT

SCENE 5

LIGHTS UP IRVING's office.

DIZZY
Okay, Lipschitz, I've got questions, and plenty of 'em.

IRVING
Dizzy please, call me Irving.

DIZZY
Great, Irving. Call me Miss Norman.

IRVING
Haven't you been married 12 times?

DIZZY
None of them counted. My name recognition trumps 'em all.

IRVING
I can see why they moved on…

DIZZY
I'm a star of the first magnitude. They're still talking about my movie, HONEYMOON AT MIDNIGHT.

IRVING
That was followed by HONEYMOON AT BREAKFAST, HONEYMOON FOR LUNCH, and HONEYMOON FOR SUPPER. None of them made a dime and you know it.

DIZZY
HONEYMOON FOR DESERT would have been the biggest of all, if the director hadn't gone on a diet.

IRVING
You say the reviews were in bad taste? But if you believe the sweet ones, you gotta believe the sour ones, too. I remember that one. They said the worst part of the movie was when the projector started. The best part was when the film broke. And if you'll remember, the critic who wrote that was your sister.

DIZZY
Ex-sister.

IRVING
You can divorce your sister?

DIZZY
You've got some nerve talking. *(looks around station)* Is this your pinnacle of success? Hitching your wagon to my star?

IRVING
I've hitched my wagon to bigger asses than you.

DIZZY
Well, I never!

IRVING
Well, you did at least twelve times.

DIZZY
Four, but who's counting. And what do you care, anyway? I'm here to do a job, slumming it, but this isn't what my agent promised.

IRVING
I resent that. WPDQ stands for the best and brightest in entertainment. A lot of big names got their start here.

DIZZY
And I'm gonna get my end . . .

IRVING
Ever heard of Heddy Lamar, Lawrence Olivier . . .

DIZZY
But he's from England.

IRVING
To work here, the boat ride over was worth it. Ever heard of Edgar Bergan, Jimmy Durante, Jack Benny, or your namesake Desi Arnez.

DIZZY
My name is Desdemona Norman, and you know it. Only my friends call me Dizzy.

IRVING
And with your attitude, you can count friends on one finger.

DIZZYI
(*muttering*) I'll show you one finger! (*full voice*) Answer me this, Irving. I need top billing, name above the title, payment in advance or you can find another star to float your sinking ship.

IRVING
Those aren't questions, those are demands.

DIZZY
Semantics. Exactly the same, only different.

IRVING
All the A-list stars turned me down. That's why we asked you.

DIZZY
How dare you!

IRVING
Take it up with your agent. You've already signed the contract, baby, so live with it. Don't even think about phoning it in. I have a lot riding on this – a lot of us do – so this isn't all about you. For once in your life, think about somebody else.

DIZZY
Nobody has ever talked to me like that. Except for . . . (*unseen, BARRY enters and watches from sideline*)

IRVING
Then it's way past time. (*exit*)

DIZZY
(*left standing there*)

BARRY
Hard day?

DIZZY
Hard life.

BARRY
I know the feeling.

DIZZY
Do you?

BARRY
Come on cupcake, I knew you before you were Dizzy. Remember?

DIZZY
I can't remember before I was Dizzy. How sad is that?

BARRY
Try harder. You always get what you want, if you set your mind to it.

DIZZY
Not always . . .

BARRY
It's good to see you.

DIZZY
(*surprised*)

BARRY
No, really. I know I was your first husband. But was I your first love? There's a difference.

DIZZY
(*no answer*)

BARRY
Your career was your first love, wasn't it? I can see it now. I couldn't then.

DIZZY
You always knew me better than anyone. I thought you'd understand. I never meant to hurt you, hurt me. Hurt…us. Life happens.

BARRY
Life happens is just an excuse. Those were the 16 happiest months of my life, followed by the 16 worst years of my life.

DIZZY
But your career took off, too! And I saw all the arm candy dripping off you at each appearance.

BARRY
Arm candy's sweet while it lasts. But I always preferred Red Hots.

DIZZY
You used to love my red hair.

BARRY
The color you have now looks almost natural.

DIZZY
You have the nerve to criticize my hair. Did you borrow that rug you're wearing from Cheetah?

BARRY
(*laughs, takes it off*). You're right. We're both way past pretending. Scary to be real, when our whole career is based on make believe. But some things are worth the risk.

Spotlight

KINDA FAMOUS

(DIZZY & BARRY)
HEAD FULL OF DREAMS, HEART FULL OF HOPE
CRAZY-SMART SCHEMES . . . THOUGHT WE COULD COPE.

BACK IN THOSE DAYS WE WERE ABLE

(DIZZY)
AS BIG AS HEPBURN

(BARRY)
OR GABLE

(BOTH)
BROUGHT OUR A-GAME TO THE TABLE
KINDA. KINDA.

(DIZZY)
I SWOONED WHEN YOU PLAYED THE LOVER

(BARRY)
AROUND MY DRESSING ROOM YOU'D HOVER

(BOTH)
SOMETIMES WE'D HAVE TO RUN FOR COVER
KINDA. KINDA.

(BARRY)
I WANNA GO BACK
I REALLY DO.
I WANNA SHARE A LINE
OR TWO WITH YOU.

(DIZZY)
WE'LL GET BACK IN,
JUST YOU WAIT AND SEE,
WE'LL MAKE A SPLASH,
CUZ IT'S MEANT TO BE.

(BOTH)
WE'RE HEADED RIGHT BACK TO THE
BIG TIME REAL SOON.
AND ONCE AGAIN
ALL OF THE FANS WILL SWOON.
WE'LL HAVE THEM HOWLING
AGAIN AT THE MOON.
KINDA. KINDA.

SELLING OURSELVES TO THE MASSES,
DIRECTORS WON'T TAKE NEW CHANCES.
THESE DAYS ALL WE GET ARE PASSES.
KINDA. KINDA.

WE'VE BEEN FAMOUS BEFORE, WE'LL BE FAMOUS AGAIN,
WHEN THEY OPEN THE DOOR, WE'LL HAVE A NEW PLAN.
WE'VE BEEN FAMOUS BEFORE, WE'LL BE FAMOUS AGAIN.

(DIZZY)
AUDACIOUS!

                        (BARRY)
                        TENACIOUS!

(BOTH)
OUTRAGEOUS, NOT SO AIMLESS,
COURAGEOUS, OFF HIATUS,

(DIZZY)
BACK TOGETHER!   (BARRY)
                        FINALLY FAMOUS!

FINALLY FAMOUS   AND BACK TOGETHER.

BACK TOGETHER   FINALLY FAMOUS,

FINALLY FAMOUS   AND BACK TOGETHER

FAMOUS
AGAIN.   AGAIN.

Start to embrace, but ROSIE interrupts & takes BARRY away, leaving DIZZY alone. SPOT off.

SCENE 6

Lights up in STUDIO, with 3 stand mics already in place.

PEARL
Okay, folks, make this rehearsal count. Remember, Wiladine has drummed up a live audience to attend.

IRVING
As opposed to a dead audience? I still think that's a mistake. The magic of radio is imagining the characters. But what do I know? Go ahead, Benny.

Sultry voice, slow song intro jazz under announcer

ANNOUNCER/BENNY

Now it's time for another exciting episode of Steve Rimfire, Private Detective.

STEVE/BARRY

It was a slow day in the office. I hadn't had steady work for six weeks. That's the way it is for a gumhead.

PEARL

(loud whisper) Gumshoe! Sorry, sometimes Benny's Underwood gets sticky.

DIZZY

Ew.

STEVE/BARRY

Gumshoe, Private Eye. P.I. Private dick. Undercover guy. I was drinking old coffee. It looked and tasted like shoe polish. Wait…I think it was shoe polish. Cordovan. Just then I heard a knock at the door. *(nothing happens)* That's right a KNOCK at the DOOR.

ROB

(doorbell rings) Sorry.

STEVE/BARRY

I mean doorbell.

ROB

(Knock-knock-knock)

STEVE/BARRY

Then SHE walked in.

ROB

(clump-wump, clump-wump) Whoops, sorry. That comes later. *(high heels walking)*

DIZZY

(glares at ROB) You did that on purpose.

STEVE/BARRY

Her legs were long and white. Like spaghetti *(mispronounces word)*. Her neck was straight and firm like a breadstick. And her hair was the color of parmesan cheese. You're right, I hadn't had lunch, and this was one hot dish of pasta. I could tell she was class by the Mogen David color lips, and her sparkly ankle bracelet that spelled out HOT STUFF. "Hi," she said, with a voice husky enough to pull a dog sled. What can I do for you, sweetheart?

CLEMMIE/DIZZY
(*uses her famous "Dizzy Girl" character voice*). My name is Clementine Fernapple but my friends call me Clemmie. I need your help.

STEVE/BARRY
What seems to be the problem?

CLEMMIE/DIZZY
My husband's taken it on the lam.

STEVE/BARRY
What's the beef. (*aside*) Damn I'm hungry.

CLEMMIE/DIZZY
You probably know about him. Harvey Fernapple, heir to the popsicle-stick fortune.

STEVE/BARRY
Eskimo pies?

CLEMMIE/DIZZY
No, they just stick it to them.

STEVE/BARRY
I don't get it.

CLEMMIE/DIZZY
Oh, are you fresh out? I've got order forms right here . . .

STEVE/BARRY
Hang on, let me get my secretary here to take notes. I can't take notes myself anymore, since the accident. (*waits for her to ask about it, and nothing*). The accident. I was severely injured. I was a hero even…

CLEMMIE/DIZZY
I want to ask you a question.

STEVE/BARRY
Well. I was working on a torpedo boat. Or maybe a tramp steamer. All of a sudden this load of . . .

CLEMMIE/DIZZY
No, I mean what's your secretary like? Can she be trusted?

ANNOUNCER/BENNY

Miss Ermangard Titwillow was a knockout with luscious lips, bouffant red hair, and an hour glass figure, with time running out. Her shorthand brought men to their knees, and women to tears. A thesaurus was not her friend.

ROB

(*Clump-wump, clump-wump, clump-wump*)

ANNOUNCER/BENNY

Ermangard always bought two pairs of shoes since one foot was a size and a half larger than the other.

ERM/POLLY

Hey youse guys! Ya snuck in on me, didja? (*to boss*) Whatja want?

STEVE/BARRY

Ermangard, take a note.

ERM/POLLY

(*poses and sings an arpeggio*)

STEVE/BARRY

Not that kind of note. Where's your steno pad?

ERM/POLLY

My what? Oh yeah, them things is expensive. I dun ran through three of 'em in the last eight months.

STEVE/BARRY

Why so many?

ERM/POLLY

I gotta stuff three under the short leg on my desk, just to keep the typey-writer from sliding off. (*bats eyes, finds a pad, searchers hair for a pencil, and poses*). I'm ready. Fire away. I mean, not with your rosco, your heater, your blue steel baby, your equalizer… I just want ya to shoot off yer mouth.

STEVE/BARRY

Clemmie, give me the full story.

CLEMMIE/DIZZY

Well, it's like this. I found out Harvey wasn't on the up and down.

PEARL

Up and up.

CLEMMIE/DIZZY
(she sits then stands up) Up and down.

PEARL
No, the line is "ON THE UP AND UP."

CLEMMIE/DIZZY
(tosses hair) You'd think being the popsicle-stick king would be enough, supplying craft supplies to vacation Bible School projects, but it wasn't. He wanted more. Fudge-sickle sticks. Eskimo pies. And the real prize, medical tongue depressors. He borrowed money from the wrong fellas. A guy who's connected, if ya know what I mean.

STEVE/BARRY
I could use a good connection.

ROB
Couldn't we all… *(reading same magazine BENNY tossed at DOTTIE earlier. It has big picture of ROSIE on cover.)*

ERM/POLLY
Could you repeat that, honey?

CLEMMIE/DIZZY
What part?

ERM/POLLY
Everything after, "Well, it's like this . . . "

STEVE/BARRY
So what do you want me to do?

CLEMMIE/DIZZY
First, could you stop all the pounding and construction going on down the hall?

ROB
(puts down magazine, starts pounding, construction sounds)

CLEMMIE/DIZZY
Find him. Just find him. He's got the account numbers to all our savings, and I'm not going to the Big House, the Rock, Stir or any of those low rent places with him. I'd rather be beat with a horse . . .

PEARL
(runs in, scribbles on script)

CLEMMIE/DIZZY
…beat with a hose? Oh, hose, yeah, I mean hose.

STEVE/BARRY
Just about then I heard the phone ring.… I heard the phone. Ring. Making a ringing sound. Who could mistake that sound.

ROB
(spoken) RINNGNGNGNG.

STEVE/BARRY
(pretends to answer phone) Are you serious? It can be. I've got her right here and she'll never believe it! This is astounding…

ANNOUNCER/BENNY
We interrupt this episode of STEVE RIMFIRE, PRIVATE DETECTIVE for a special announce—

(PHONE really rings)

ROB
Hey, it wasn't me that time.

SCENE 7

BOB
(enters excited, wearing Hawaiian shirt, straw hat) I have an announcement to make. *(looks around)* Where is everyone? Get everybody in here. Where's Rosie, she needs to here this, too.

DIZZY
Who knows where she is, that sneaky son-of-a-

BARRY
You promised to be nice.

BOB
The deal is a done deal, we did it. The deal that is. I want to tell you about the new station owner. *(looks around)*

WILADINE
You sold the station? Bob, I'm so happy for you…and Rosie. Your happiness makes me happy. *(a beat)* I'll go get her for you.

BOB
Wait, honey. Rosie already knows. This news is for us, not just me. I've already put a deposit on a cabana in Cuba. A little bird told me your secret dream. Pack your sunglasses, the ship sales in two days. (*they embrace, he looks around*) What?

WILADINE
Honey, they're waiting for the announcement . . .

BOB
Oh, right. Drum roll, please. The big money magnate Mr. R.P Walter has bought WPDQ-Radio.

PEARL
Wait a minute. Did you say R. P. Walter?

ROB
(*sound effects when ROSIE and DOTTIE enter*)

BOB
Yes, Mr. R.P Walter. Here's Rosie, his assistant! She's been on the inside, and convinced R.P. to invest. Thank you, little lady!

ROSIE
(*enters*) Hey kids, it's been a kick getting to know you.

WILADINE & DIZZY
(*look at each other*) His assistant?

DOTTIE
You fibbed to us, sneaking around all the time. You never told us. (*to BOB*) And you're still fibbing. Rosie's not any assistant at all. This is R. P. Walter herownself. (*runs to ROB and snatches magazine*). You're Rosie the Riveter, the power woman of the decade!

BOB
Wait. YOU are R.P. Walter? I just sold WPDQ to a *woman*?

DIZZY
Welcome to the world of entertainment.

BARRY
Be nice. Try, anyway

ROSIE
Getting to know you, being treated like one of the gang made all the difference. You are the reason I decided to invest in WPDQ, and the future of television.

ROB
Philanthropist? I could use an investment.

ROSIE
I was born into money. But when he was alive, my husband ran the show—our lives, our investments, even named the Poodles after his favorite stars.

DOTTIE
I knew that. It's here, in my investigatory notes.

POLLY
Poodles?

DOTTIE
Peck, Bogie, and Garland. *(points to notes)*. See, girls can be good investigatory reporters, too! And philanthropists. *(looks around)* You all thought she was a man.

ROSIE
We never had kids. Radio was my life, until television came along. Now I have a chance to make my own decisions and investments. Welcome to WPDQ-Television.

> *ROB plays chime cue and ALL sing the new jingle. ALL FREEZE except for IRVING and PEARL.*

IRVING
(off to one side) Where does that leave me? I mean us? *(to PEARL)* We've been sold to television? No one knows anything about television. The only thing I know for sure is that if television ever comes in, it'll be like radio. Free and it always will be.

PEARL
Do you see the big picture? You can direct! Benny and I can write! No one knows what the hell they're doing in television anyway, there are no parameters. It's perfect timing for those willing to jump off that cliff.

IRVING
I just don't want to splat.

POLLY
(*breaks freeze for line, then freeze again*) Pedro wouldn't recommend it.

PEARL
What choice do we have? This is the money in the suitcase that everyone dreams of. (*pause*) Do you know that you're my favorite director?

IRVING
How many directors do you know?

PEARL
(*long pause, looks at him directly*) Only one.

IRVING
Do you know you're my favorite writer?

PEARL
How many writers do you know?

IRVING
(*counts on fingers*) I don't know, 15, 18, maybe 20.

PEARL
Really? You're not blowing smoke? I mean, Uncle Bob says stuff like that when he can't pay me.

BOB
(*ALL un-freeze*) Payday's no longer my problem.

IRVING
I don't smoke. I think this is the beginning of a beautiful relationship.

ROSIE
We'll use the existing studio, of course. But we need a director (*ignores IRVING*), sound technicians (*ROB waves hand*), camera crew, and talent of course. (*looks at DIZZY*) I've already talked to your agent, and he says you're available.

BARRY
That's great!

DIZZY
(*finally thinking about someone other than herself, to BARRY*) But we're a package deal.

ROSIE
He's already in, Dizzy. Don't get mad, he had a nondisclosure. We needed a name commodity with great presence and acting chops to represent our A-list product line.

BARRY
I'm the new face and voice of SHINOLA SHOEPOLISH.

DIZZY
I'm in!

IRVING
Me, too! (*they look at him*) You said you need a director? Here I am!

ROSIE
Yeah, I've seen your work.

IRVING
Thanks! But what about a script?

ROSIE
Pearl already gave me her treatment for our first big show. It's great! It's innovative! It's killer-diller material!

BENNY
It's co-written. (*to PEARL*) Okay, you can have top billing.

IRVING
Did everyone know about this but me?

DOTTIE
I figured it out cuz of my investigatory skills. But I'm still looking for my dream job. Won't television want investigatory news reporters, too?

ROB
Dottie, you could help me with sound effects. I could teach you. After all—girls can do anything men can. Right?

ROSIE
I've been watching you, Irving. Other than Wiladine—who's sailing into the sunset with Bob—you're the glue that holds this crazy WPDQ family together. And I need someone like you keeping me on track. (*to DOTTIE*) And someone like you with a nose for innovation and good a story. So will you stay on, and take the job?

SNAZZY
(bursts in) I just got the biggest sponsor that WPDQ ever had! Ever hear of AT&T?

ROSIE
You got American Telephone & Telegraph?! They're huge!

SNAZZY
No. I got Al's Truck & Towing! They're even bigger! *(to POLLY).* Setting my copy to your musical jingle did the trick. *(BARRY pays off the bet)*

RADIO DAZE

(WILADINE)
GOT MY PIECE OF PARADISE

(BOB)
I'M NOT MUCH TO BRAG ON

(WILADINE)
BUT DANG, IT'S NICE.

(PEARL, BENNY, IRVING, ROSIE)
GOT CREATIVE CONTROL,

(DOTTIE, ROB, POLLY, SNAZZY)
I WAS ON A BAD ROLL,

(ALL)
WHEN A NEW VISION
CAME ALONG.

NOW WE'RE HANGIN' ON

(MEN)
IT'S NOT JUST A PHASE.

(ALL)
WE'RE HANGIN' ON,

(WOMEN)
FLEXIBILITY PAYS.

(DIZZY & BARRY)
IT'S FOR CERTAIN WE'RE DESERVIN'
STATUS QUO IS OVER TURNIN'
WE'LL KEEP LEARNIN'
FROM RADIO DAZE.

(MEN)
I'M HANGIN' ON

(WOMEN)
IT'S NOT JUST A CRAZE.

(MEN)
WE'RE HANGIN' ON

(PEARL, BENNY)
LET US WRITERS REPHRASE.

(ALL)
IT'S FOR CERTAIN WE'RE DETERMINED
TO KEEP EARNIN'

(ROSIE)
I'M CONFIRMING
WON'T TORPEDO
YOUR RADIO DAZE.

(ALL)
WE'RE HANGIN' ON
OUR CHOSEN FAMILY STAYS.
WE'RE HANGIN' ON,
FLEXIBILITY PAYS.

IT'S FOR CERTAIN WE'RE DETERMINED
NOW WE KNOW THE TIDE IS TURNIN'
WE'LL KEEP LEARNIN'
FROM RADIO DAZE.

CURTAIN

MUSICAL NUMBERS

ACT 1

WPDQ JINGLE (Various)..93-94

RADIO DAZE (Irv, Benny, Bob, Wila, Pearl, Dottie)......................95-99

HUNTING FOR MY MUSE (Pearl)..100

SPONSORS (Wila, Dottie, Rosie)...101-106

SNAZZY MALONEY (Snazzy, Barry).......................................107-109

KINDA (Barry)...110-111

FAMOUS (Dizzy)..112

MAKE A DIFFERENCE (Benny, Ladies)..................................113-115

RADIO DAZE (Company)..116-117

ACT 2

WHEN I MET YOU (Wila, Bob)...118-119

NEWS FLASH (Dottie, Company)...1209-123

SISTERS.(Polly, Rosie, Wila)..124-125

PARTNERS (Pearl, Benny)...126

KINDA FAMOUS (Dizzy, Barry)..127-129

RADIO DAZE (Company)..130-133

1. WPDQ-JINGLE

Amy Shojai/Frank Steele

Amy Shojai/Frank Steele

2. Radio Daze

Amy Shojai/Frank Steele

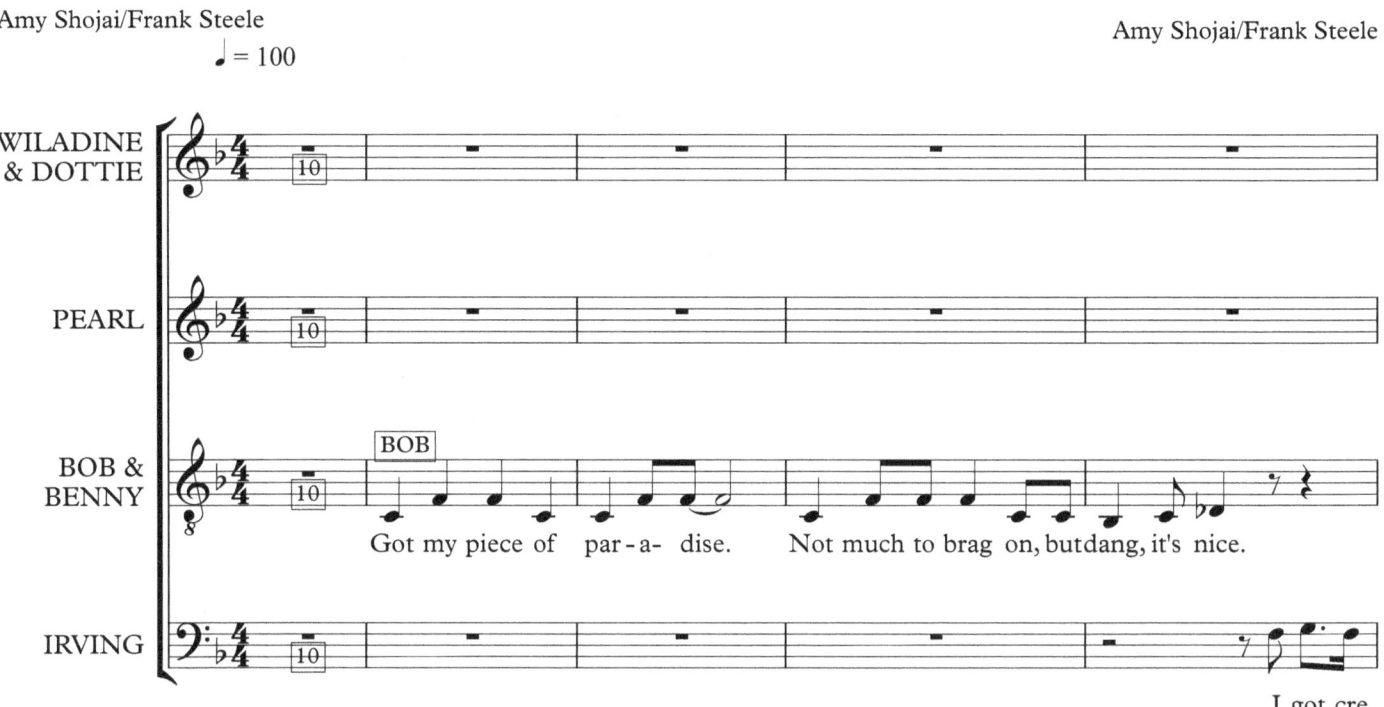

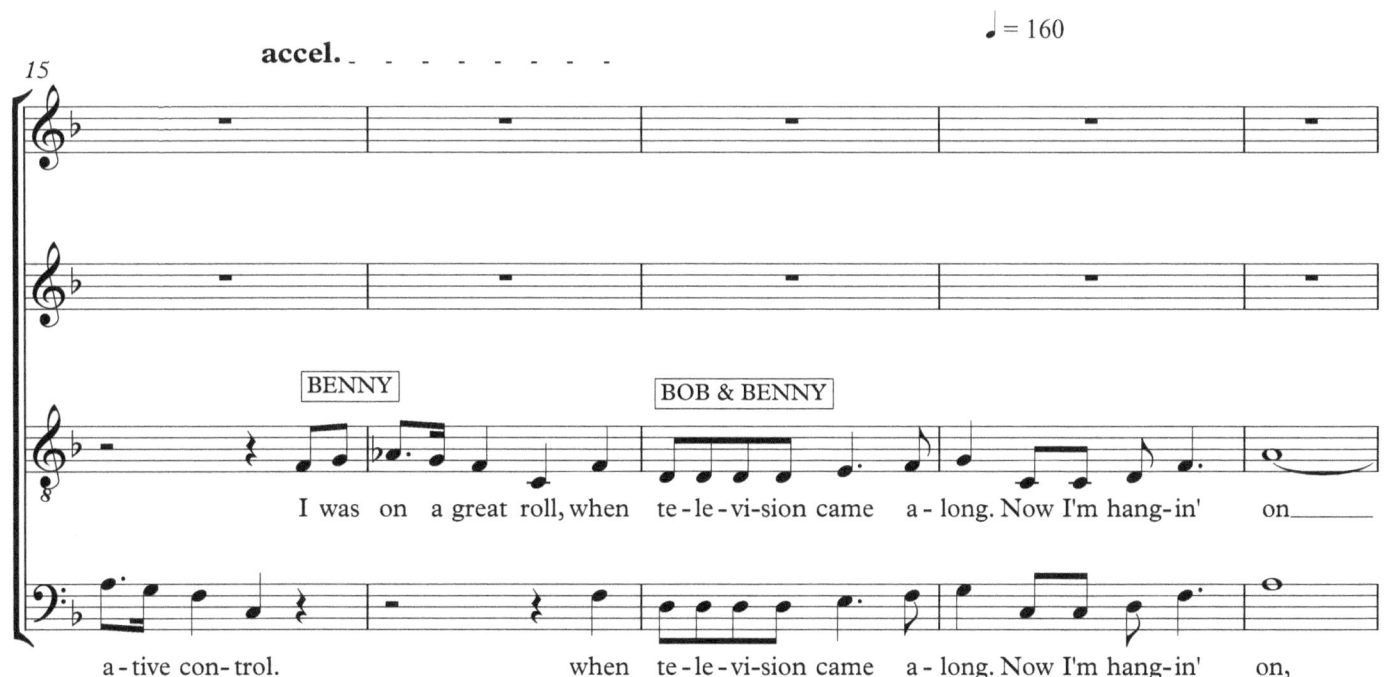

Copyright © 2018 Shojai & Steele Plays

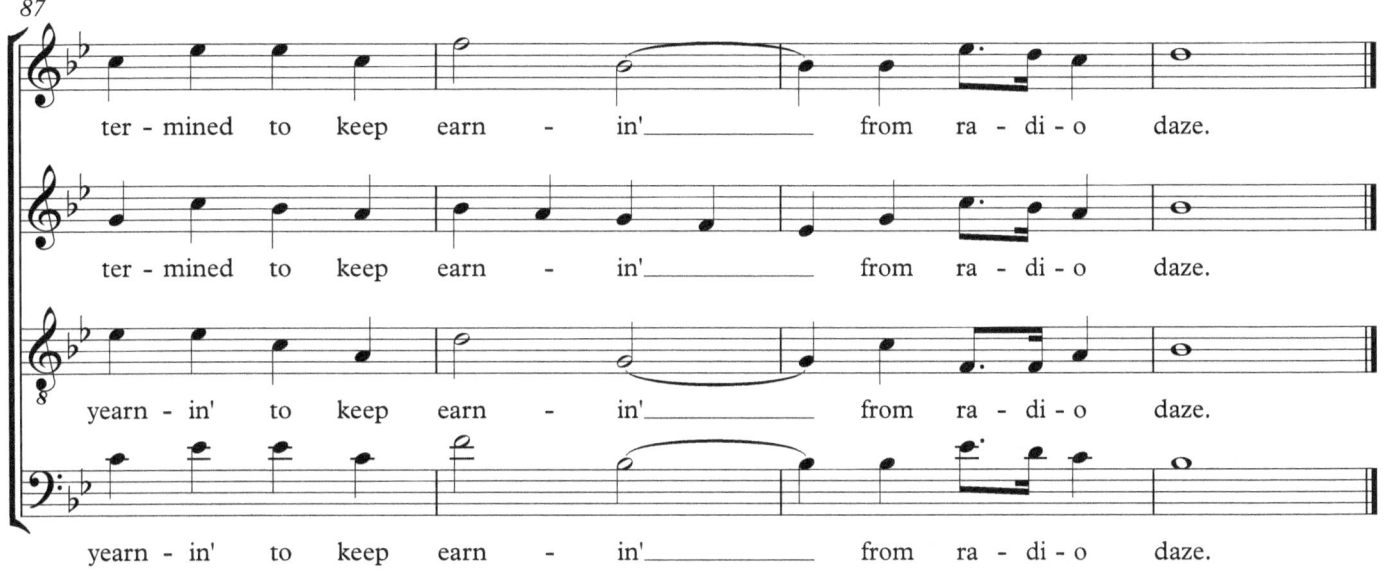

3. Hunting For My Muse

Amy Shojai/Frank Steele

Amy Shojai/Frank Steele

Copyright © 2018 Shojai & Steele Plays

4. Sponsors

Amy Shojai/Frank Steele Amy Shojai/Frank Steele

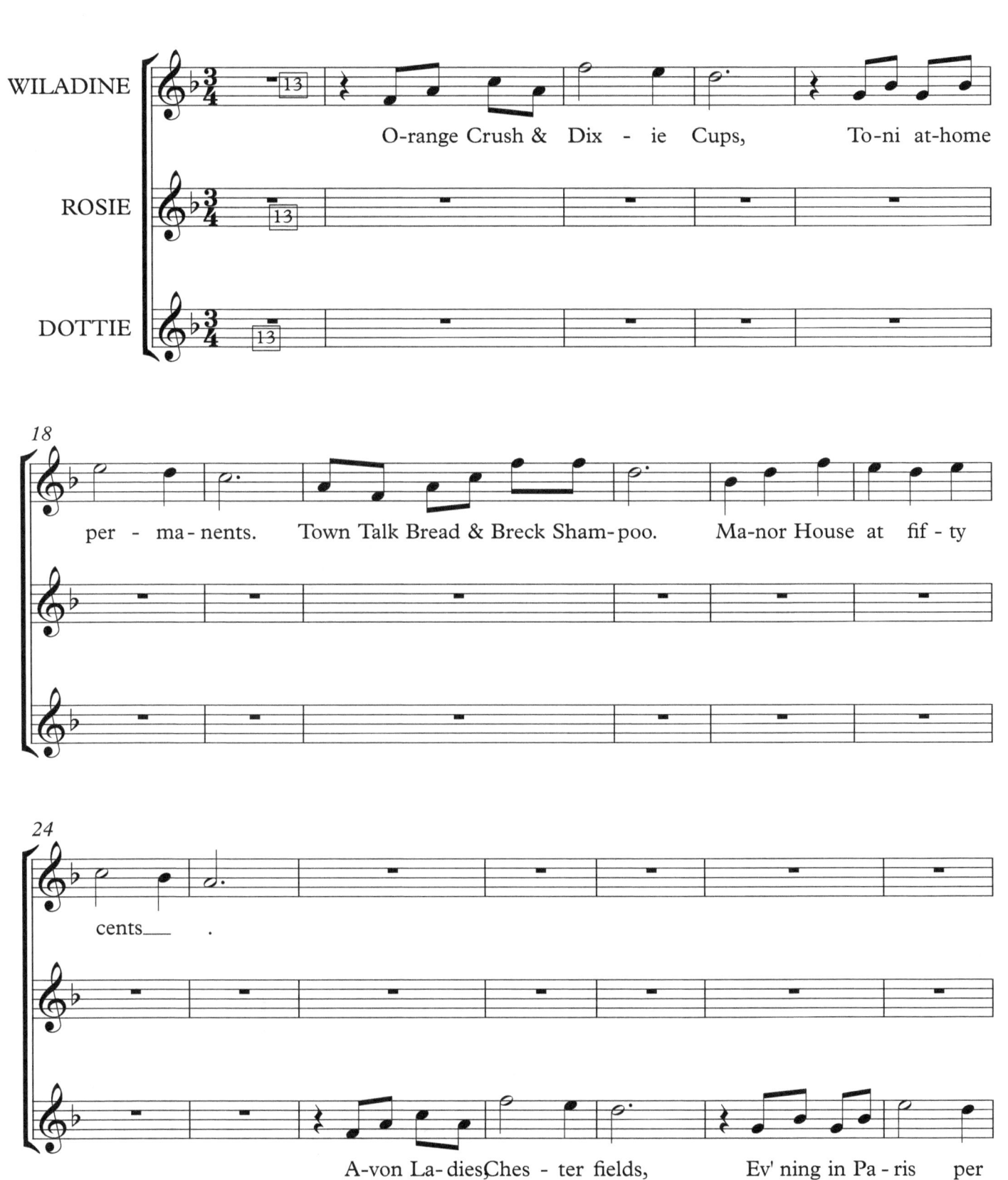

Copyright © 2018 SHOJAI & STEELE PLAYS

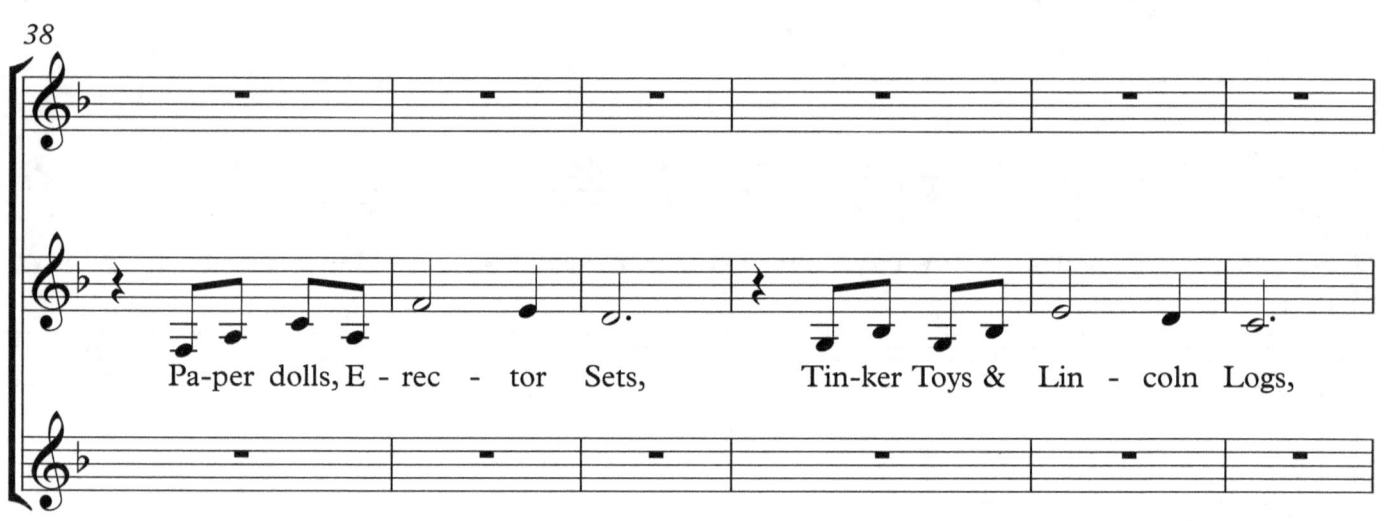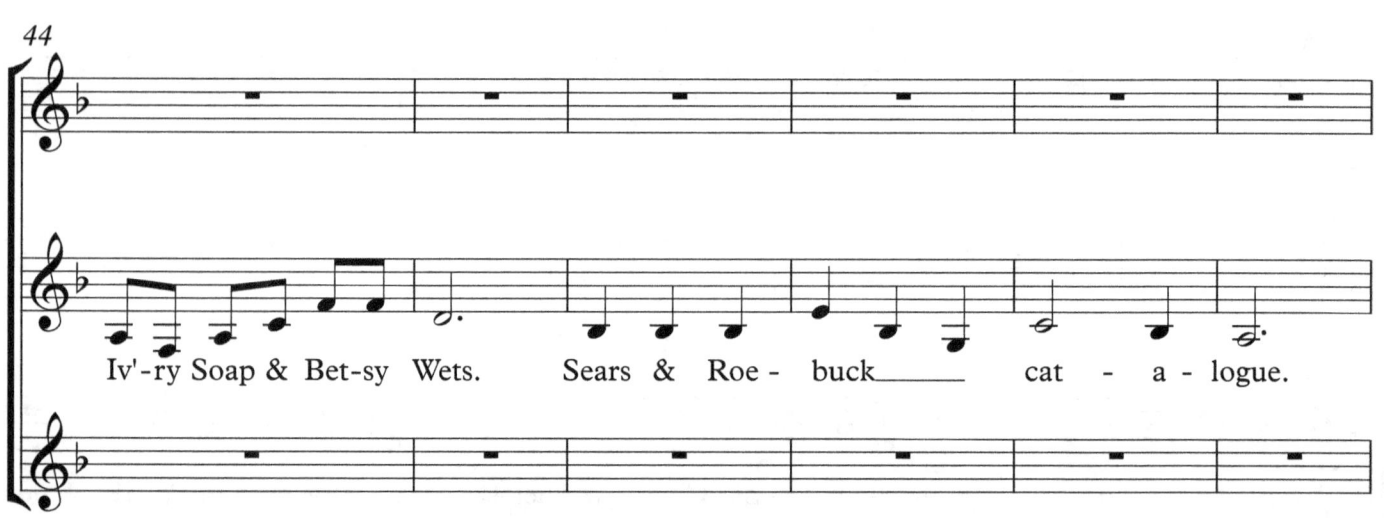

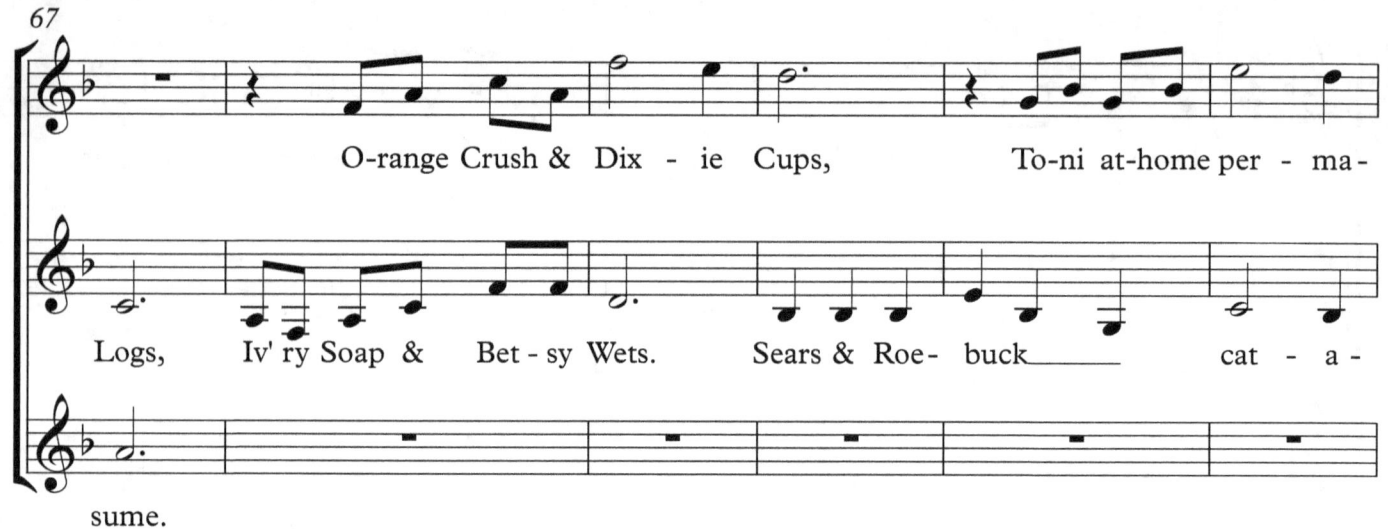

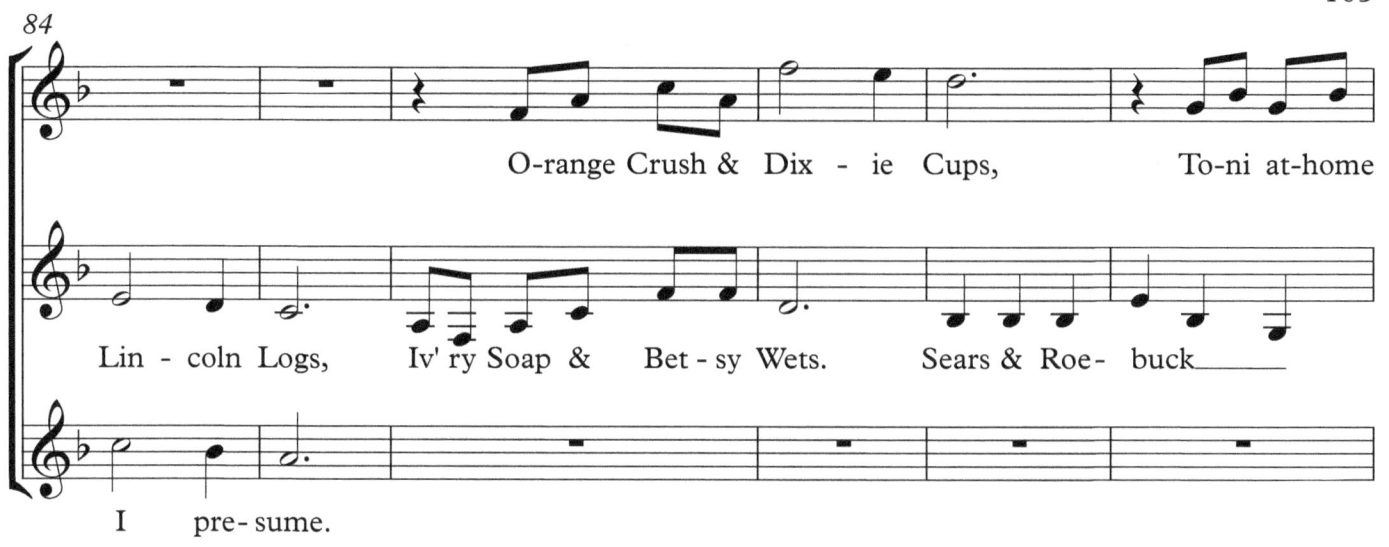
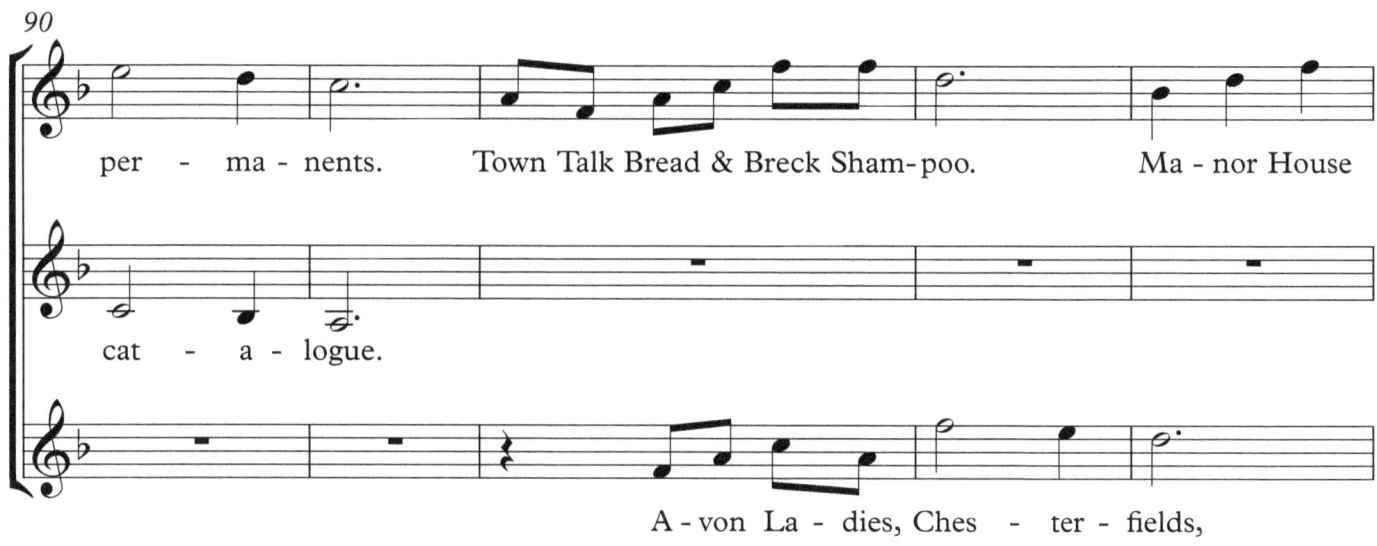
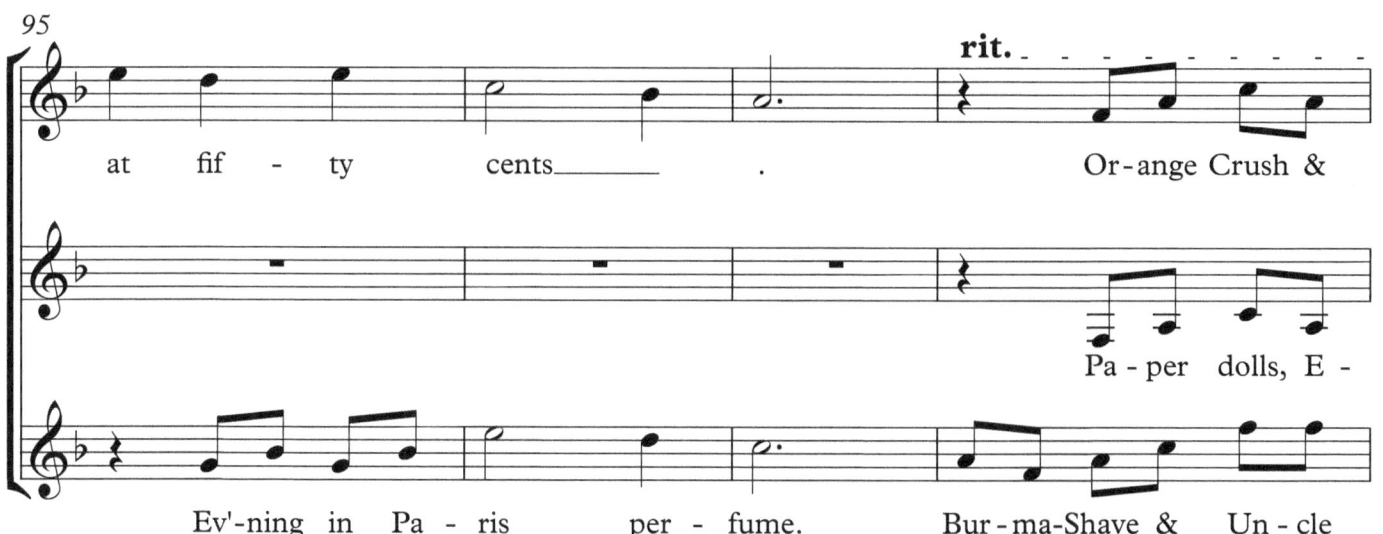

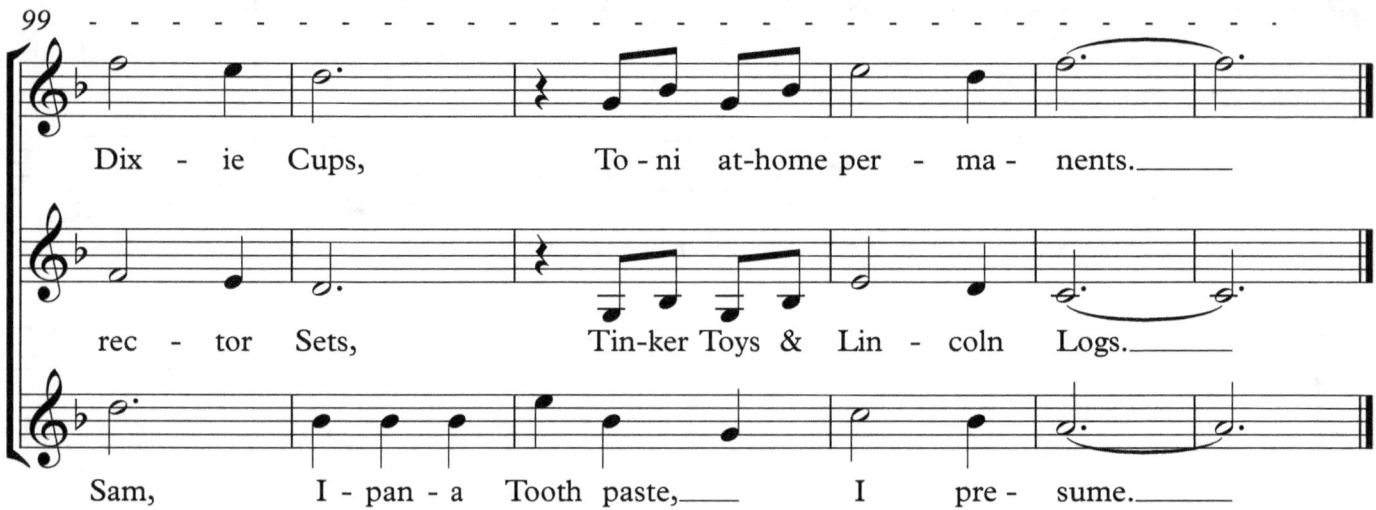

5. Snazzy Maloney

Amy Shojai/Frank Steele
♩ = 130

Amy Shojai/Frank Steele

Copyright © 2018 SHOJAI & STEELE PLAYS

108

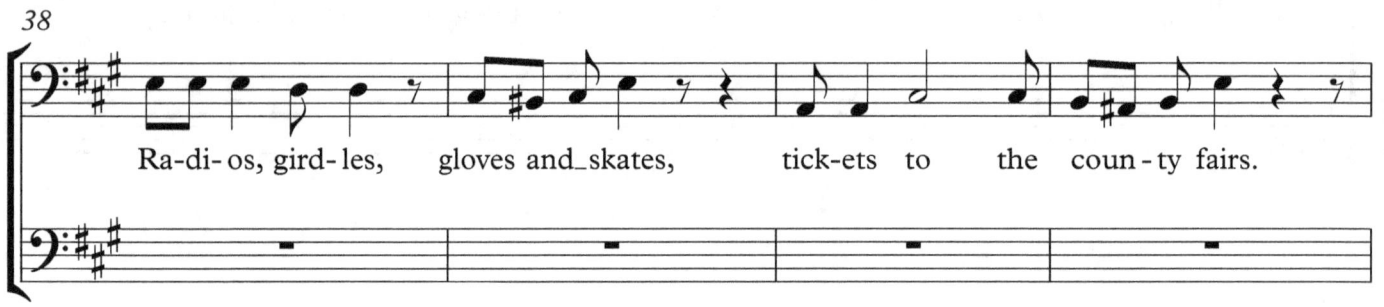

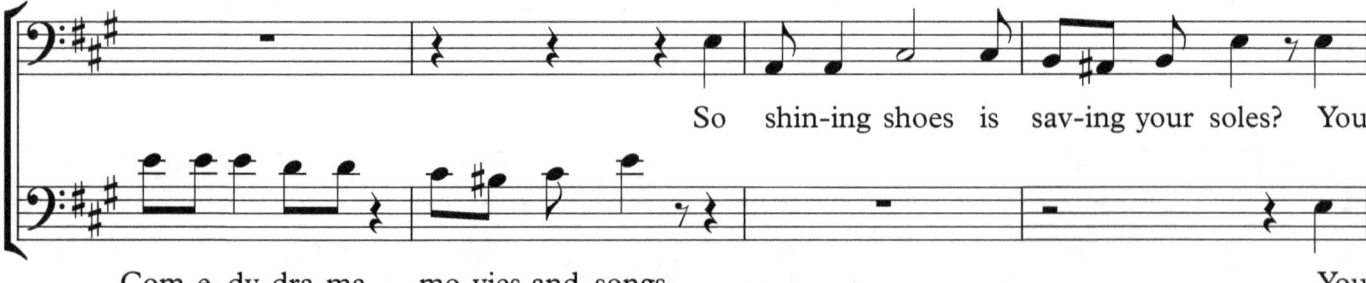

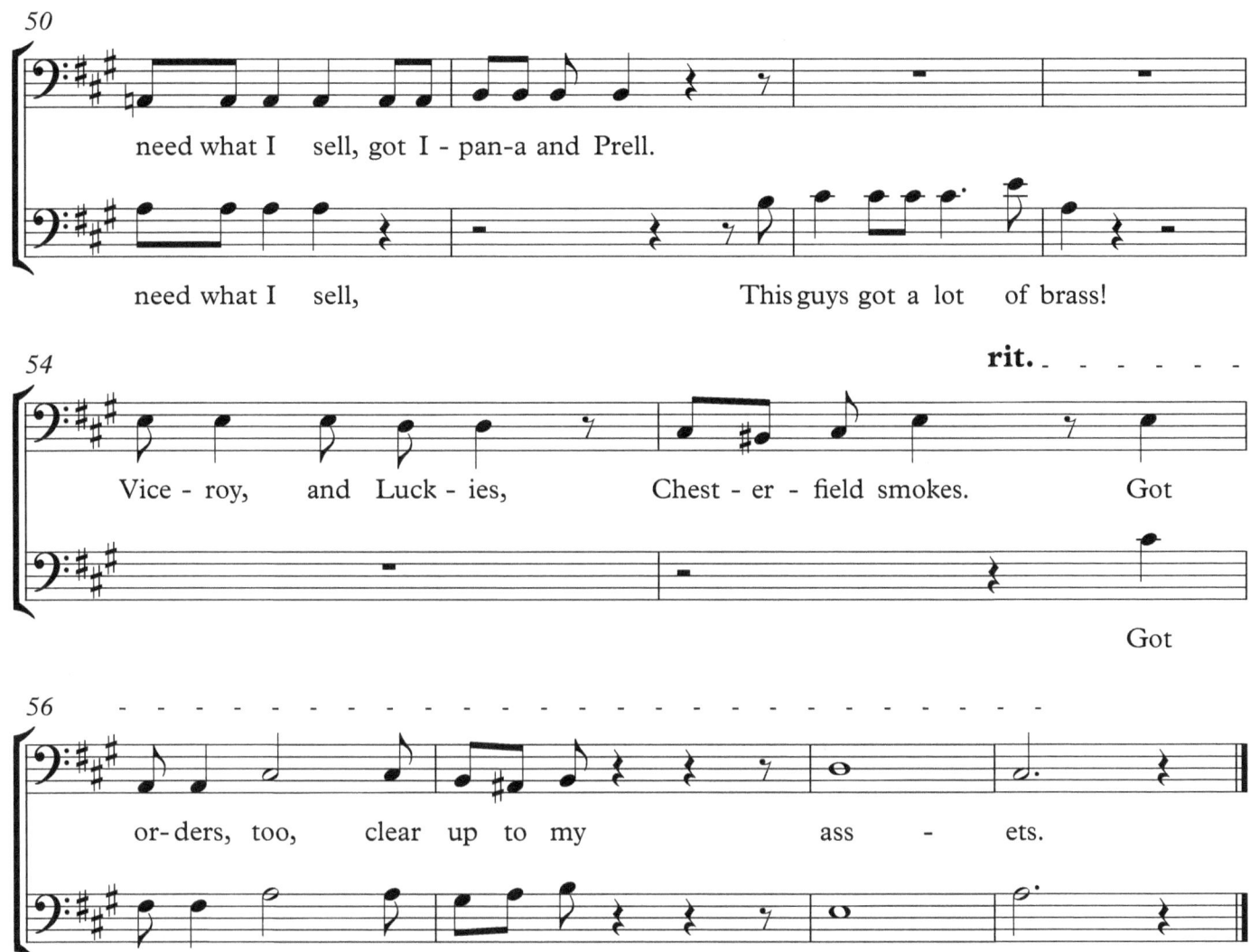

8. Make A Difference

9. Radio Daze

Amy Shojai/Frank Steele

Amy Shojai/Frank Steele

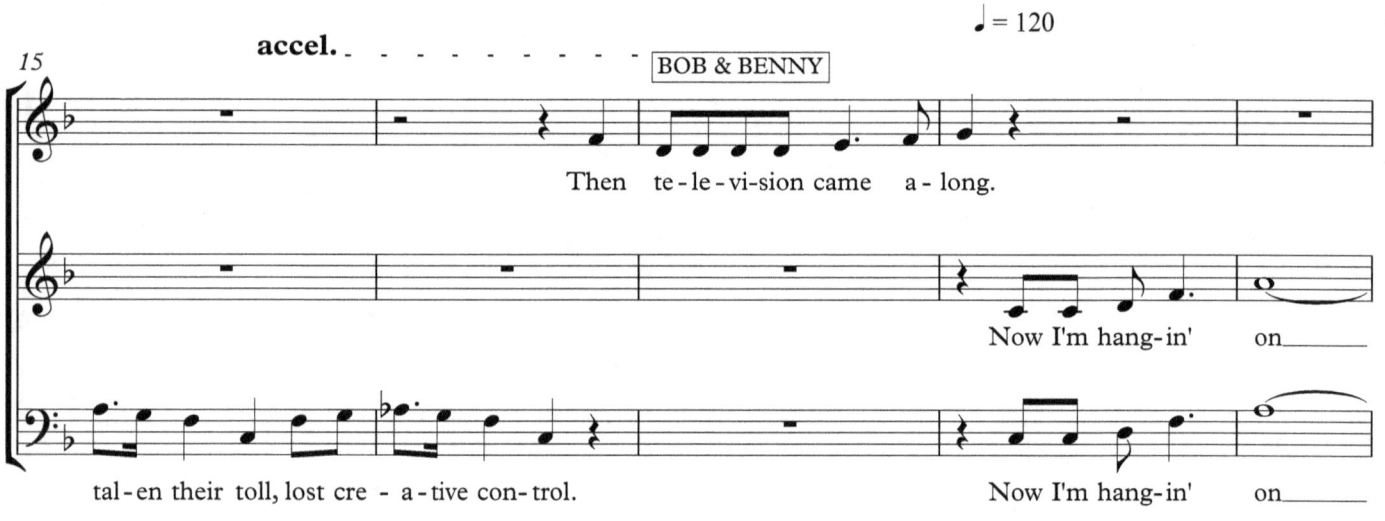

Copyright © 2018 Shojai & Steele Plays

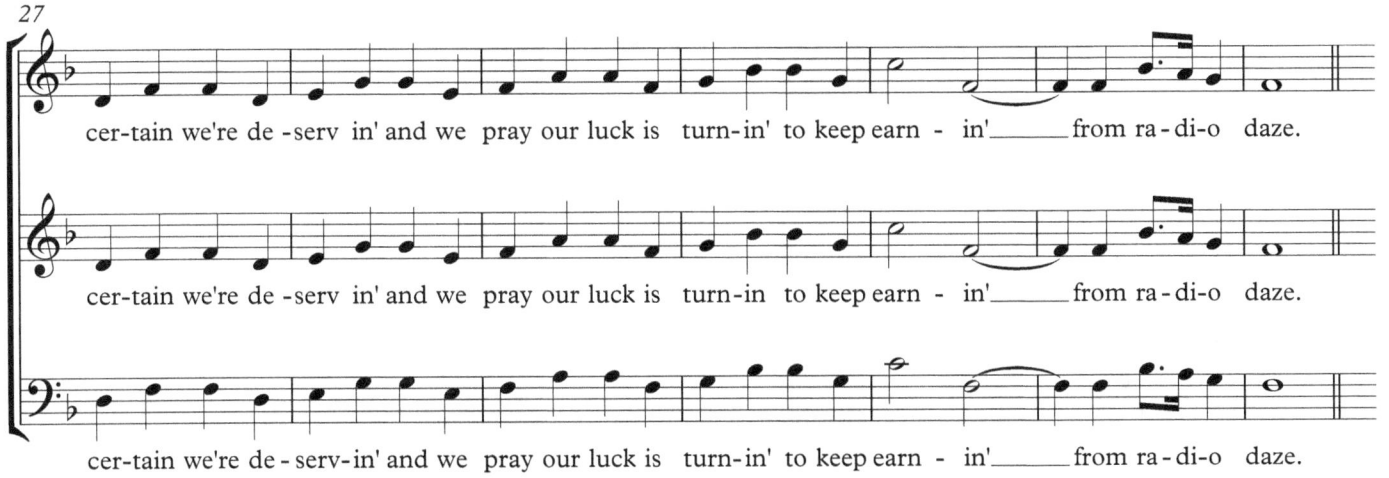

11. News Flash

Amy Shojai/Frank Steele

Amy Shojai/Frank Steele

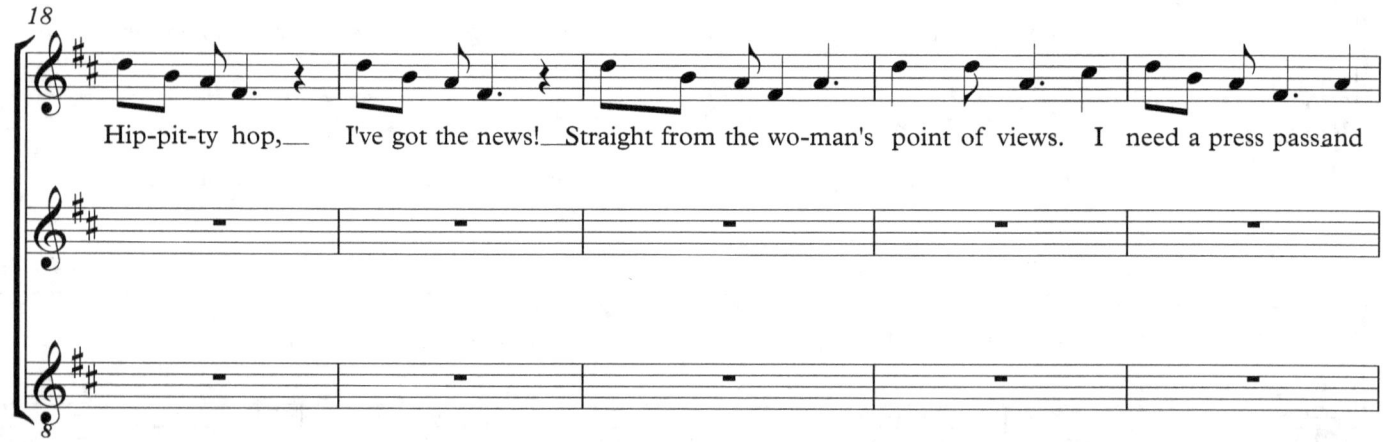

Copyright © 2018 SHOJAI & STEELE PLAYS

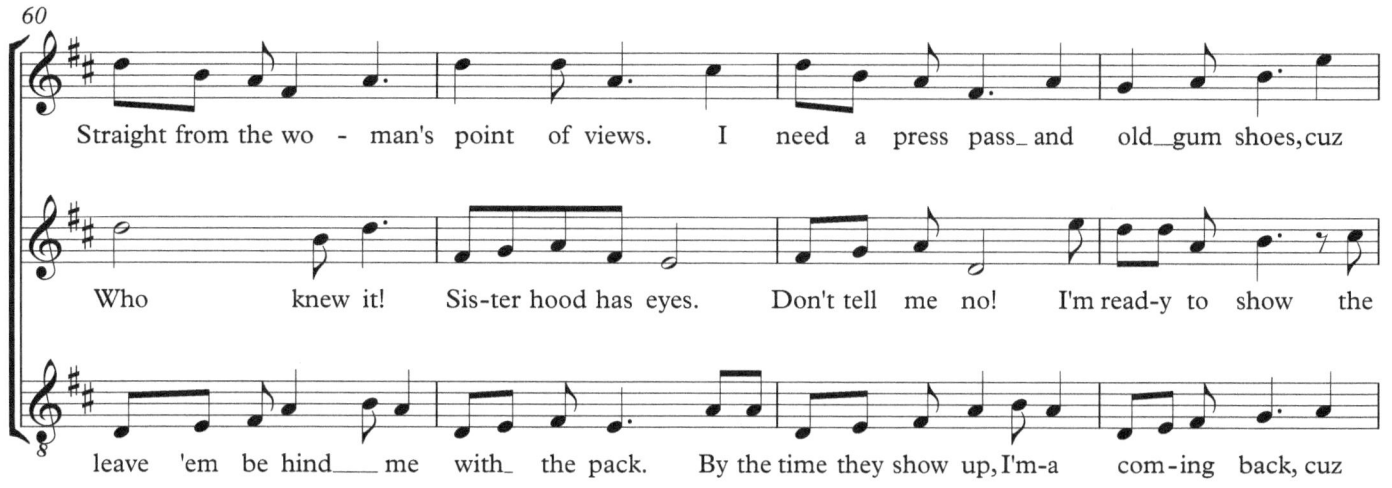

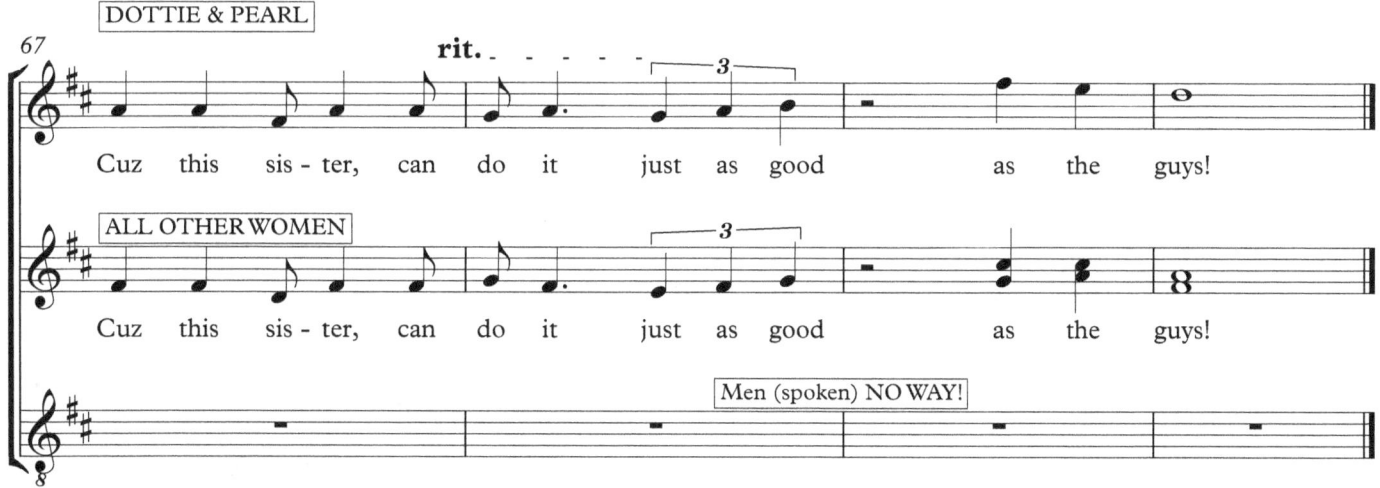

12. Sisters

Amy Shojai/Frank Steele
Amy Shojai/Frank Steele

POLLY

♩ = 150

Show biz called, and we was bit.
A-gents, bills, and jeal-ous-y caused
Ne-ver looked back, not once. Made it big in no time flat, in
man-y a sleep-less night. Sing-ing busi-ness lost its charm, each
on-ly a few short months.

♩ = 100

One bad sis-ter makes you bit-ter,
sis-ter thought she was right.
two can make you blue. Three to-geth-er ain't no feath-er in your cap.
Four that whisp-er cause a blist-er hurts you ev'-ry day.
You can't choose, some-times you lose it in a snap

♩ = 150

Pe-dro met a hor-rid fate, o-ver the falls in a vat.
Pat-ty and Pan-sy they took it real hard when Pe-dro took to sea.
Did-n't plan it ver-y well to land on the rocks in a splat!
Both left the biz on the arm of a guy leav-ing the songs to me.

If we'd stuck to sing-ing our songs, it

Copyright © 2018 Shojai & Steele Plays

13. Partners

Amy Shojai/Frank Steele

Copyright © 2018 SHOJAI & STEELE PLAYS

15. Radio Daze

Amy Shojai/Frank Steele Amy Shojai/Frank Steele

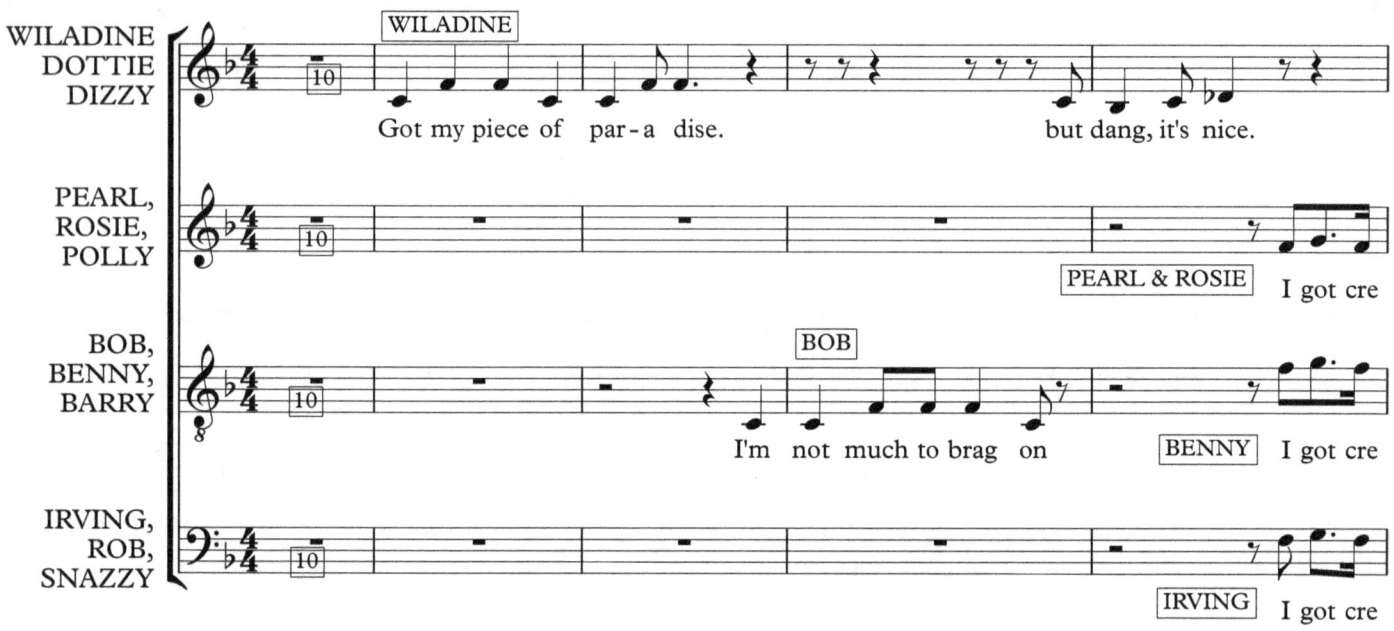

Copyright © 2018 Shojai & Steele Plays

www.ingramcontent.com/pod-product-compliance
Lightning Source LLC
Chambersburg PA
CBHW081723100526
44591CB00016B/2485